Bag it all

as told to

Suman Chhabria Addepalli

Bag it all

as told to
Suman Chhabria Addepalli

The inspirational story of an entrepreneur who built a 100-crore company with the power of intent and love

NINA LEKHI

JAICO PUBLISHING HOUSE
Ahmedabad Bangalore Bhopal Bhubaneswar Chennai
Delhi Hyderabad Kolkata Lucknow Mumbai

Published by Jaico Publishing House
A-2 Jash Chambers, 7-A Sir Phirozshah Mehta Road
Fort, Mumbai - 400 001
jaicopub@jaicobooks.com
www.jaicobooks.com

BAG IT ALL
ISBN 978-81-8495-981-9

First Jaico Impression: 2017

Page design and layout: Special Effects, Mumbai

Printed by
SAP Print Solutions Pvt. Ltd.
28 A, Laxmi Industrial Estate, S. N. Path
Lower Parel (W), Mumbai - 400 013

This book is dedicated to my Guru, Shree Rishi Prabhakar,
and also to the love of my life, Manjo.

— Nina Lekhi

Foreword

The first time I met Nina Lekhi at her modest office in Lalbaug, I was taken by surprise.

The CEO of Baggit walked into the office wearing a simple blue and black cotton shirt. And she said, "Give me ten minutes."

She did not proceed to take an important call, or answer an urgent email. She sat down – right in front of me – to meditate.

When she opened her eyes, there was a soft glow in her face. A contentment rarely seen in the frantic world of business.

I included her remarkable story in my book *Follow Every Rainbow*, which is about women entrepreneurs. The title of her chapter was 'Peace, Love, Business'.

Four years later Nina called me out of the blue and I was once again taken by surprise. In a short span Baggit revenues had zoomed from ₹ 34 crore to over ₹ 100 crore.

Nina shared the secret of this growth – following the principles of Siddha Samadhi Yoga. Both in her personal and professional life.

So when Nina told me that she wanted to write her autobiography, I agreed to assist her.

Fortunately, by then I had begun a company that helped people like Nina tell their story as biographies and memoirs. So through us, Nina met Suman – the talented writer who penned down Nina's thoughts.

Nina's story has so many beautiful lessons, which need to be told to this generation. Firstly, academic success is not a be-all and end-all. Nina failed in her 11th class exam and that gave her the burning desire to prove herself. She started a small business while still in junior college, that became the company we know as Baggit today.

Qualities like perseverance, hard work and following your passion matter more than marks.

Never let anyone stick a label on you that says 'stupid'. You were born to do something – figure out what that is. And you will never look back!

Another thing I admire about Nina is her ability to be a 'Lakshmi'. A woman who is the heart and soul of the business and has also involved her family in it – to scale up and grow. Wherever there is family, there is some friction, but Nina has managed to give each one his space – and his due.

Lastly, I think Nina's story makes it clear that spirituality is not something you plan to do 'after retirement'. It is something you practice in everyday life. Spiritual awareness gives you the strength to release negative emotions in a non-toxic manner. Making you a better, more sensitive human being. And a more effective leader.

Whether you are an entrepreneur, an employee, a working mom, a student or a housewife, you will find something in this book. To make you think, make you smile, make you wonder.

That is the power of a story – to give you the inspiration to rewrite your own.

Rashmi Bansal

Prologue

I spend three days of my week in Katarkhadak, near Mandi Lake, 180 kms from Mumbai. Sitting in a tree house, sipping cups of herbal tea, with all the reports, documents and designs that need my attention, I complete my work in one-third the time it takes in Mumbai.

Sometimes I look into the distance and wonder, "How did all this happen?" Never in my wildest dreams did I imagine that one day I would be the Managing Director of a 100-crore company.

I was just a mischievous middle-class kid. I was not academically brilliant. At the same time, I am not some phoenix who has risen from acute poverty. I lived the good life; as a daughter in a culture where girls were generally told to 'take it easy' until they get married.

Such was my complacency that I earned the dubious honour of being the only student in class XI – probably the only student *ever* – who failed the foundation course in art. My world seemed to come to an end when I was not allowed to attend college for a year!

I started my business to fill up the year that I lost

at college. My father called my first set of canvas bags '*thelas*' to carry vegetables. But that did not deter me.

I was married at 22 and that did not stop me either. Luckily, my husband, Manjo, and my in-laws were always supportive.

I was never an obsessive businesswoman. I simply loved my work and the process of creating trendy products. What I have enjoyed the most is working with people who are my family and who have become my family. The attrition rate at Baggit is practically zero.

Our beautiful daughter, Vedoci, was born after 12 long years of marriage. Motherhood overwhelmed me. I wanted to spend more time with my growing daughter than with my growing business. I was eventually able to do both by using some simple techniques that I learned along the way.

This year, Baggit completes 25 years, and, in the world of business, it is a success story. But let me tell you a secret – this success has been the outcome of an inner journey. The same inner magic that I tuned into when I failed at college kept me afloat through business and personal challenges.

Siddha Samadhi Yoga (SSY) is the cornerstone of my life. My Guruji, Shree Rishi Prabhakar, the founder of the extremely powerful SSY Program, transformed me from a 'party animal' to a loving and giving human being. This, in turn, has transformed our business.

In the five years since we started using SSY techniques in the workplace, our sales have grown fourteen-fold. Yes, this really is possible and I have shared the 'why' and the 'how' in this book.

I hope this book helps everyone who has ever doubted themselves, or wondered if they are good enough. There certainly have been times when I have.

Life is really very simple if you believe in yourself, and in others. This faith is more vital to a business than having strategic investors, an MBA, or a limitless marketing budget.

If you *believe*, anything is possible. You really can 'Baggit' all.

Nina Lekhi

Contents

1

Give Me One Problem, God

I was the youngest brat of a nuclear Sindhi family – the typical *hum do humare do* set-up.

My dad, Lalchand Punjabi, had moved to Mumbai from Pune in the 50's with empty pockets. He slept on the streets and did odd jobs.

Eventually, he would go on to become a full-on entrepreneur.

Along with his brothers, he bought a huge factory building in Andheri. He produced customized gears and sprockets for oil and cement mills. The market was tough and worked on credit, but dad never made us aware of his struggles. He had a bad temper, probably because of this stress. He lacked patience and yelled a lot at the servants, though never at the family. My mother Gita always says that I've inherited his looks as well as his temper.

> "Even as kids, I could see her Taurean bull-headedness. At 16, she told me that one day we would become hotshot independent women who will travel the world. And we did!"
>
> *— Rita Lekhi,*
> *Nina's childhood friend and sister-in-law*

My brother, Mukesh, was – and still is – a very easy-going and loving person. As far as I recall, there was no struggle growing up. Whenever there was an argument between him and me, it was my poor brother who was yelled at. I always used my 'puss-in-boots, innocent-young-sister' expression to my advantage!

Mom was a full-time homemaker until I was 12. After that, she became a disciple of Guruji Sant Ma Braj Deviji, and wasn't home much. She attended daytime *satsangs* and would be away from 3 pm until dinnertime.

My dad did not forbid her involvement with the ashram, even though her absence forever changed our routine at home.

Though mom was not at home between 3 and 9 pm, she always knew what was happening with each one of us – like any working mother today.

People often ask me whether I was affected by her absence. The answer is no. There was no doubt we missed

Nina with her father Lalchand Punjabi, mother Gita Punjabi and brother Mukesh year 1978

her; but because my father did not make a fuss about it, neither did I. My brother and I became more responsible and took charge of the house. That made us really confident as kids.

I realized that there were financial pressures when dad did not hire a full-time maid. That is why I ended up cooking meals for the family.

I recall studying for exams during the day and preparing dinner in the evening. My *rotis* broke like *papad*, and I often served burnt *dal* mixed with sticky rice, but everyone ate my culinary disasters quietly. They had no choice.

My father often discussed business matters at the dinner table: the problems he faced in his factory, with his customers and with funds. Any other girl might have gotten bored, but I lapped it all up. I thank my dad for teaching me these 'business *fundas*' – it's the closest I would ever get to an MBA!

My family was a bit unusual, but, even so, I was a regular, happy-go-lucky girl. Growing up, I was full of life and mischief. Eighteen of the twenty boys in my class had a crush on me – though I must add that there were only two girls in my class at Greenlawns High School, Worli. I was also the head girl of the primary section. You can guess how overconfident that could make a kid.

"Nina was very pretty and extroverted. She also spoke as if she were on stage 24/7. Every word had so much of acting and excitement. The whole of Worli would know if she ever won a game of cricket, whereas, in comparison, Mukesh would not inform me even if he stood first in class."

— Gita Punjabi,
Nina's mother and Trustee,
Ma Braj Devi Ashram, Vrindavan

I have always been a 'people person.' I loved to socialize and spend time with my friends. But my parents were protective and mom never allowed sleepovers. Whenever I wanted to go out for a party, I'd have to convince dad that it was my friend's birthday. The same birthdays used to come twice or thrice in a year!

I'd return home from these parties, sometimes even at 3 am, to see dad in the balcony waiting for his daughter. I always believed that I had fooled him. It was only when he passed away last year that mom told me that he always knew.

What he did for me, I can't even imagine doing for my daughter.

We lived in a beautiful and safe gated colony that had three tall and three short buildings. When I was about 12-years-old, a strange man met me and my friends (Champa, Duru and Rekha) on the stairs of our building. He said, "You know that show on TV, I can get you a role for it." We were so naïve that we believed him!

So he started meeting us every day on the stairs and taught us the funniest *filmi* dance steps. I was totally thrilled and one day accidentally blurted out to mom how I was going to be on T.V. She spat out her tea in shock. Without another word, she confronted that man, slapped him and took him to the police station. That was my first lesson in knowing whom to trust.

Thereafter, mom ensured that I was busy with dancing, cooking and even stitching classes. In my free time, I played cricket with my cricket-crazy brother. I somehow managed to get him out with my *gasar-gundi* style of bowling. You know how little sisters always have their way of making sure they don't get out!

Late evenings, I just had to do something creative. I must have inherited that gene from my mom. She is fantastic in arts, crafts, drawing and painting – so much so that my friends in school were always finding ways to convince her to do their charts.

I used to visit a stationery shop in my neighbourhood daily to buy cellophane, art and glazed paper. Mom and Mukesh would join in the fun when they had the time.

The walls of our home were testimony to our in-house talent.

Mukesh has always had an eye for design and, till date, leads the design team at Baggit. I think he's the only man in the world who actually loves shopping.

As busy as I was during the week, my weekends were *vela*. I spent my time cycling through the breezy green lanes of Worli sea-face. This is a passion that continues today. Cycling introduced me to my first boyfriend, another Sindhi fellow. He used to play cricket down in the building's garden.

We stayed on the sixth floor of a beautiful sea-facing apartment, and I used to study in the verandah, so that every time he hit the ball high, he would look up at me. And I looked down at him. That was the way I studied. Obviously I didn't remember much during class tests.

My life turned topsy-turvy when I joined the Breach Candy branch of my school. The Worli branch had classes only till the sixth standard and we had no choice but to move.

It was a new world for me. I was shocked to see the super hip SoBo (South Mumbai) crowd at Breach Candy. From being the head girl and teacher's *chamchi*, I became a nobody. From hearing 'Nina-Nina-Nina!'

on everybody's lips earlier, I only heard 'No-No' when I looked for acceptance into new groups!

But it was here that I met Rita Lekhi, my best friend and guide. We introduced ourselves with some awkward staring-and-instant-hatred sessions. But soon we became close, to get even with the boys in the class. Everything that I learned at that age, from handling myself in public to handling boys to handling work situations, I learned from her.

Until I met Rita, I was this *behenji* who shopped at Fashion Street. I was famous for being the short girl with long, elastic waist cotton skirts. I didn't know how to buy fitted clothes, even though I was extremely fit. Once Rita entered my life, I learned what it means to be cool. I learned how to party, how to live and how to shop. What more could a teenager want?

And so my school days continued – both blessed and monotonous. Most people pray to God to solve their problems. I was probably the first to pray for at least one problem!

No wonder God noticed! He decided to give me a kick on my well-toned ass.

I always knew that the creative side of me would thrive only in the field of art. I took admission in the prestigious

Sophia Polytechnic's Foundation Course, majoring in Commercial Art and Design. Free from the restrictions of my school life, I was eager to explore the wild side. I made new friends, quickly dusted off the 'good girl' tag and began bunking lectures. I tried smoking, drinking and doing weed, and watched every movie that released, first day first show. I did it all!

I discovered new best friends, Debbie and Devangi, on the first day of college. We got along because we were all crazy. On our first day, we said, "Let's bunk!" It was 1983, and the Barbra Streisand movie *A Star is Born* had just released. We bunked class to see it. The next day, we bunked again to watch the same movie. On the third day nobody went to college. All of us met directly at the theatre! After that we never did our drawings. Just before submission, we would cough up some incomplete assignment.

Not surprisingly, my wish for a problem was granted. I received my first-year mark sheet and, to my horror, I had flunked the Foundation Course. In Commercial Art! Nobody flunks in painting.

This was a very big deal for me. I was not the kind of person who fails. From being head girl of primary school to failing in college was unacceptable. And in art! You know, everyone understands if you don't pass the CA Entrance, or can't crack high *funda* entrance tests to the IITs. But flunking a bloody painting exam was totally embarrassing. I still remember the horror of being the *only one* in class who had failed. I couldn't speak. I took my mark sheet and walked home. That A4 sized sheet was like a zero-capabilities stamp. One year of indiscipline made everyone else in my class superior to me.

> "Nina hated crying in front of others, but this was such a blow that she couldn't stop the tears. I clearly remember her walking out of college without saying a word. We were too young to be sensitive towards her in the way she needed it. That day, we realized the gravity of what we all had done during class hours. I think all of us grew up in that moment."
>
> *— Devangi Parikh,*
> *Nina's classmate at Sophia Polytechnic*

My failure was a tight slap. I wanted to prove to myself that I wasn't stupid. What you feel inside is what you think others feel about you too. I felt that everybody thought I was a loser. Even worse, I could not attend college for a year and could return only to re-take the exam. That's when I decided to do something productive with my free time.

I enrolled in part-time courses at Sophia Polytechnic.

The only ones available were screen-printing and interior designing. I joined both. Since I had a few hours to spare between classes, I took up a job as a sales girl at Mike Kriplani's. He ran a *salwar-kameez* retail store near Sophia.

I worked hard to numb the memory of failing, and my courage set the course for the road ahead. All through this period, mom and dad were very sensitive towards me. I was only 17 and it was clear to them that I could not stomach my failure. In retrospect, I was really lucky to have such wonderful parents. Had they shouted at me, my self-esteem would have sunk lower. Because they did not blame me, I became responsible and found my own way.

LEARNING:

The only way forward, is forward.

Failure has that power to distance all that was once dear to you. My classmates wouldn't touch me with a barge pole. I had two options. I could either sit at home crying over spilled milk, or look ahead. I stopped thinking about my failure and focused on the future. I learnt everything about running a retail store in the same year that I had lost everything.

Had Cinderella turned back to pick up her shoe, she wouldn't have become a princess. The very barge pole my friends didn't want to touch me with... I used to vault myself into a new future.

2

My Marriage and My First Retail Outlet

Phase 1 of Baggit: 1984 – 1988

So, I had failed. I was hurting inside and wanted to prove my worth – more to myself than anyone else.

Since both the screen-printing and interior designing courses at Sophia were part-time, I had a lot of time to kill after class. I joined as an intern with Mike Kriplani. He was a retailer of luxury *salwar-kameez*. Within a few months of work, I learned everything about inventory management. Thereafter, I joined Shyam Ahuja who was a retailer of carpets.

Interns were not paid much then. I would spend my stipend on cab trips from college to the store. Both Mike and Shyam would laugh at me and ask, "Why are you working?" I told them I was eager to learn. The truth was

I wanted to remain occupied and not have too much time to dwell on my failure.

The upside was that both internships taught me the A-Z of store management.

Weekdays were packed with work. Recreational activities continued on weekends. My school friend, Mona, and I regularly swam and played badminton at the NSCI club in Worli. We carried separate bags, one for each activity: a gym bag, a swimming bag and a partying bag. Buying a high-quality, feminine bag, even for college, was a huge struggle. For us, bags were basic needs, not luxuries. We had noticed during our shopping sprees that you could find cool t-shirts with slogans and one-liners, but not cool bags.

"Every bag that Nina made at home would sell at full price. I have never seen any piece unwanted. The year she failed at Sophia's, post dinner, she would sit on the dining table, creating designs on large sheets of paper. I would say goodnight to her, and wake up next morning to see her there, still working!"

— Mukesh Punjabi,
Nina's brother

Mona and I began discussing the idea of making the kind of bags that we liked – bags with attitude. Thus started my experiments with designing bags.

This was in 1984, and my 'office' was one half of the children's room at my dad's two bedroom flat in Worli. That room was supposed to be my bedroom but I slept on the swing in the living room. The space where my bed should have been became my workplace, filled with cartons, designs and other material.

Even before the first lot of bags was stitched, Mona and I had zeroed in on the brand name. We were swimming late one evening – just before she left for the United States – singing Michael Jackson's 'Beat it' when the perfect name occurred to us.

The name was *Baggit*.

> "She was only 18 when she created the brand Baggit. It was not common then to create a local Indian brand. There was this craze for imported stuff, and besides, you needed infrastructure, money and confidence to put your name on your products. Many tried to scare her but she never allowed other people's doubts to weaken her decisions."
>
> *— Vicky Ahuja,*
> *Head of Sales & Marketing, Baggit*

We were sure it was a very cool name, inspired as it was by MJ's song. The name stuck. Shortly after, Mona left India and gave up the idea of partnering with me, but I was determined to go ahead. Every bag that I made from then on bore the Baggit name.

My business required me to visit crowded markets such as Abdul Rehman Street, Do Tanki and Hindmata, the mecca of fabric and unstitched material in Mumbai. As a teenager, I had zero experience of going to such places, far less dealing with the vendors there. My mother came to my rescue. She accompanied me to the markets and taught me how to distinguish between types of fabrics and accessories.

My mom always had the spirit of peacefully achieving whatever she wanted, within available resources. I am certain that I have my entrepreneurial spirit from her. Whenever people refer to me as a go-getter, I silently acknowledge my mother's DNA.

I borrowed ₹7,000 from mom as capital to fund my idea. Then I roped in the building liftman, the security guard, and the local zip-repair*wala*, who worked as my *darzi*. They helped me cut and stitch canvas bags.

Every day, our 'mini-factory' used to run at home from 6 pm to 8 pm. I paid them per piece. After the material was cut and stitched, we banged the buttons into the canvas. The person staying on the floor below used to repeatedly complain. "Why is there so much noise from your house every evening?"

I began all this without a business plan. Factoring in a *tagda Sindhi* profit margin, I priced my bags at ₹50-60 each. Such a reasonable price was possible since I had no overheads. Of course, I didn't factor in the rent of my Worli home-office.

That is what made those early days so special – no plan, no overheads.

My dad's mentality was always that girls have to get married and ultimately cook; so why bother! He did not value my hard work and thought it was a passing phase. On the other hand, mom always encouraged me. It was thanks to her that I had previously attended a one-month stitching class; so, while I didn't know enough to make a bag from scratch, I knew the basics of stitching. And I kept trying. I used the best materials I could afford, and designed all the bags myself. I started displaying these homemade bags at various places. First, I requested that Mike give me some counter space in his store. At that time, it was my dream to see *my* products sold there. When he agreed, I realized what a huge task it was! It required me to ferry a heavy suitcase full of my bags on a BEST bus from home to his Marine Drive outlet. I committed to bringing back what remained unsold. Astonishingly,

Nina carrying a sack full of bags for a photo shoot all on her own

almost all my bags sold out quickly!

Word spread. I got an order from Amarsons, a large department store at Breach Candy. By early 1987, I was selling almost 30 bags per month and making over ₹5000 in sales. I would happily blow this money in pubs with friends.

This wild gang I partied with every weekend included Rita, my best friend from school. We did some crazy things together, like hopping on a bus to Goa, telling our parents that we were going there for a wedding and giggling when we got caught. My mom loathed Rita, and for good reason.

With Rita came the package of her *tridev*: her three elder brothers, Dev, Sunil and Manoj. Partying and returning home late was possible only because of this trusted-trio who always dropped me home. My favourite amongst them was her youngest brother, Manoj, or Manjo as I loved calling him. We got along like a house on fire.

One night, I reached home at 3:30 am. We had been dancing at the popular discotheque 'Xanadu' at the Horizon Hotel. I kept reminding the gang that my deadline was midnight. As usual, the reminders fell on deaf ears. I knew I would get one tight slap from mom when I got home. Even though this was not the first time I was returning home so late, I was really nervous opening the front door. Before I could insert my key, mom opened

A snap of my SSY gang from the yesteryears

Nina chilling her two besties: Monica and Rita

the door. She was seething with rage. She shouted, "*Kis ladke ke saath raat-raat tak ghoom rahi hai, besharam*?" (Which boy were you loafing around with all night, you shameless girl?)

"When Manoj set his eyes on Nina, it was love at first sight. He told us she was the most beautiful girl he had ever seen. He soon proposed to her. Initially, Nina ignored him and Manjo was very put off by this. A few months later, he became very popular at college because he was quite a funny guy. Nina was suddenly interested in him, but by then he had lost interest. So, Rita played Cupid in getting them together."

— Dev Lekhi,
Nina's brother-in-law

Without thinking, I blurted out, "Rita's brother Manjo; he proposed to me at the pub!"

It was the truth. Except that the proposal had happened a fortnight ago. I had been so taken aback that I hadn't responded to him. Not because I wanted to say no, but because I was only 22 and I needed time to think about marriage.

After what I told mom, however, responding to Manjo's proposal was no longer my prerogative. Within hours, our respective parents were speaking to each other. Even though Manjo was a Punjabi and I was a Sindhi (an out-of-community marriage was never an option until then) and our elder siblings were unmarried. In fact, Manjo's mother was elated that at least *one* of her sons was thinking of settling down.

We were engaged within a week. I now had the license to party late with the gang.

My personal life was settled. Now, I focused on reaching out to bigger audiences by holding quarterly sales at Cymroza Art Gallery in South Mumbai. I also put my bags on display at Zedd's, a garment retail store owned by Manjo's family. I was a thorough professional, mind you, and I paid to use their space.

I remember every time I was in the cab with my stock, I repeatedly whispered a prayer, 'Hey Lord Krishna, I see myself having a *superb* sale, *superb* sale." I learned this concept of reframing your mind formally in SSY later, but as a kid I practiced it often. Visualizing things the way I wanted them to be always worked for me. I have always been more right-brained; visualizing came easily to me.

I remember my first big order. I received a call from

someone called Jalaal *bhai* who ran a store called Regal, in Bandra. He had come to know about our bags, probably through Amarsons. He placed an order for 200 bags! I was super excited.

Back then we had a Maruti 800. We filled the back seat with three tall cartons of bags. Mukesh drove and I was sitting in the front; we couldn't see anything in the rear view mirror. When we reached Regal, Jalaal *bhai's* man, Razaq *bhai* said, "Good stuff! Now set up the bags!"

We arranged all our bags in their shop. They were such genuine guys; they bought each and every piece for hard cash. Jalaal *bhai* opened his drawer and gave us ₹45,380! Just like that. I still remember the exact figure because Mukesh and I returned to the car, shouting in Dolby Stereo volume: "FORTY-FIVE-THOUSAND, THREE HUNDRED AND EIGHTY RUPEES!"

Manjo's business had a retail store at the Oberoi Hotel in Nariman Point (a popular shopping hub). Next to his shop, his friends, Philip and Kiran, had a garment store, which wasn't doing well. In the year 1987, they sub-let a small rack in the store to me. Mukesh and I took turns sitting there every evening. We achieved fantastic sales!

By early 1988, this counter became so successful that I appointed my first sales girl to manage it. We began to

Manjo and my first trip to Europe, five years after our wedding

look for people to scale up. I approached my cousins and friends to help me during sales, which I began holding all over Mumbai. Most of them are still with us in senior management positions.

Soon, Mukesh and I started thinking of renting a store of our own at the Oberoi mall, but the rents were stratospheric. We realized that many South Mumbai retail outlets were moving from Nariman Point to a new hub, Kemp's Corner. Actor Suniel Shetty had also opened a store called Mischief, adjacent to Cymroza Art Gallery. Suniel was the fiancée of Mana Kadri, my classmate and very close friend from Sophia. We liked a shop that was right next to Mischief, and Suniel not only got us a good deal, but also guided us on the store concept. He told us to open a full accessory store. No one else had thought of it. We liked the idea and started selling shoes and hair accessories along with our bags.

The rent of the store was ₹5000 per month and we called it INXS.

It was our baby. We wanted to make it as unique as possible. A professional designed part of the interior, but many of the ideas were ours. I had seen a shop at the Taj Hotel that had a fuchsia-pink wall. I decided to paint INXS in the same shade.

Normally, painters take stainers and mix them to get the right shade. For example, if I wanted a pinkish tone, I would take maroon and mix it with an appropriate quantity of white. But since I wanted *that same fuchsia-pink* shade, Mukesh and I took the purple stainer and painted the walls without mixing any white into it. Such enthusiasm!

My mom was shocked when she saw the colour. She kept asking me, "How can you paint a shop *so* purple?"

We stocked and set up the store ourselves, during the first few sales. The store would shut at 8 pm and, from 8 to 9:30, Mukesh and I would prepare the store

> "It was his shop. I remember Mukesh wanted his own shop since he was a child, but Nina worked for it. Even at that young age, she kept saying, this is what he wants and I will make it for him."
>
> *— Gita Punjabi*
>
> *Gita Punjabi, Nina's mother and trustee, Ma Braj Devi Ashram, Vrindavan*

for the sale. I visited the store every month to organize merchandise and create new window displays.

I was going for my wedding outfit trials during the same week that we painted the store. I had glue marks and paint all over my clothes. INXS opened in November 1988 and did very well. A month later, Manjo and I were married.

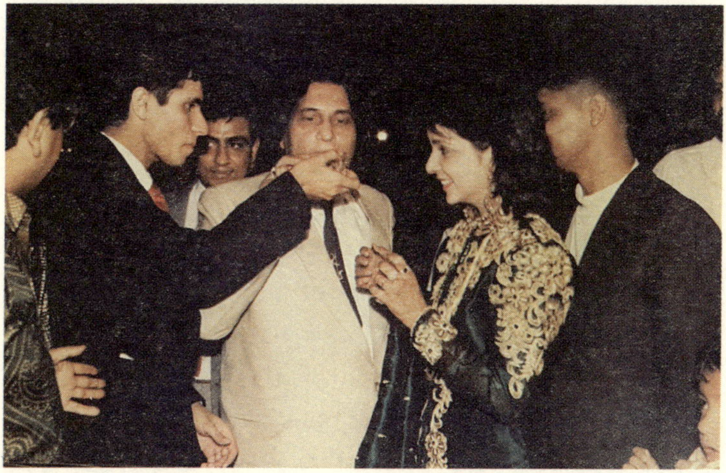

Nina and Manjo on their wedding reception with her father-in-law

My marriage was one of the best things that has ever happened to me. I was so used to Manjo's family and home that there was no change in my routine. In fact, when I look back, the only unexpected detail I can recall about my marriage is the actual wedding ceremony. I found it so strange that we were taking *pheras* at almost 2 am. Apparently, dead-of-the-night *mahurats* are common for Punjabis. But I remember worrying that the families were celebrating so much, they would forget the ceremony altogether!

My parents-in-law doted on me more than my parents. This can be such a huge source of strength for any woman, and I cannot say enough on this matter.

The year 1988 was an absolutely splendid for me. I completed the two-year Diploma in Textile Design from Sophia College and won a state award for designing an innovative bedspread. I hired my first salesgirl, rented my own retail store, and got married. I also hired Baggit's first General Manager, Sudhir Mistry, who is still with us. By the end of that year, Baggit was a serious business with an annual turnover of ₹30 lakh, growing almost 30 percent annually.

I was just 22-years-old. My hard work had redeemed me.

Nina with her collection

LEARNING:

If you are brave enough to walk the path alone, help will come in some form.

The odds may seem stacked against you, but if you swim against the current with determination, things will become easier. My dad discouraged me, but my mom encouraged me a lot more. Mona left, but Mukesh wanted to work with me. Oberoi mall was expensive but Suniel Shetty appeared with the INXS idea. Don't lose heart or hope; help will always arrive if you work hard and are committed to your goal.

3

Quality People, Quality Products

Phase 2 of Baggit: 1989 – 2001

By 1989, the demand for our bags was multiplying. The space and the number of employees in my manufacturing setup were not enough. After our wedding, I had already moved my factory out of dad's home into a loft in Manjo's *gala* in Lalbaug.

But soon this space, too, became insufficient. Then, I shifted into my dad's 740-square-feet *gala*, incidentally in the same building. This building is the Lalbaug Industrial Estate, also known as Narayan Udyog Bhavan. We fondly call it our 'Narayan Dev' because it has been so lucky for us. Nowadays, real estate agents refer to it as the 'Lekhi House' because Baggit operates from 45 *galas* in the building.

"Nina is very clear about what she wants. In the early 90s, we had this big (all-cash) buyer – India's first organized department store. They demanded higher margins and their brand name on our bags. Nina told them, 'My brand or no deal!' I shat in my pants at the thought of losing them, but to my shock, they agreed!"

— Vicky Ahuja,
Head of Sales & Marketing, Baggit

Even as we were expanding our production facility, INXS in Kemp's Corner was our only formal retail outlet. Besides bags, we stocked accessories like earrings, sunglasses, scarves and elastic belts. While Baggit was made in India, INXS also stocked Chinese goods to give customers whatever they needed.

INXS was always thronged with happy shoppers. Soon, Mukesh got the confidence to buy the store outright. We paid for only about ten percent of this deal with our own money. The rest we borrowed and repaid within five years.

We were getting repeat orders from many retailers and were constantly in the race to increase production. There were many lucrative offers to produce bags for other brands, but I did not succumb.

I insisted on producing bags only for 'Baggit,' but it was increasingly difficult for me to supervise all operations. We had to expand our team. In those days, the business was still run without too many formal systems. Recruitment was not a highly planned affair. I looked for people only as and when required.

Sapna Karkera, the sister of my best friend Medu (Mahendra Karkera), approached us for work. I hired her as a designer. She turned out to be one of our best recruits. She was with us for 14 years, eventually becoming the Head of Marketing.

> "Besides retailing at INXS, Baggit also rented a showroom at Narayan Udyog Bhavan, where retailers from all over India would come and buy. They selected designs and paid in advance. This worked by word-of-mouth, without a rupee spent on marketing. We also did not aggressively contact retailers with new samples. It helped that there weren't too many players then."
>
> *— Sudhir Mistry,*
> *General Manager, Baggit*

That's how I used to recruit. Anyone who wanted to work and anyone who could get the job done was welcome. I did not care about qualifications. It was only for the design team that I judged whether the recruit had good taste, as reflected in their sense of dressing.

Mukesh was clear he did not want to join my dad's business. He had seen my father struggle with long credit cycles. He wanted to work with me full time and do business in hard cash. I still needed trustworthy people to join us, especially during sales. We held sales every quarter, all over Mumbai. I requested my cousins to manage these 15-day long events and paid them on a per-day basis.

My cousins, Vikas (Vicky) and Vishal Ahuja, were still in college then. They spent their evenings at their respective fathers' offices at Lamington Road. Everyone knew that they did not do any work there. Vicky, in particular, would reach his dad's office, have a cold drink, and go home.

They were always there for me, however, when I reached out to them. Their reliability fuelled my growth.

One day in 1990, I went over to their homes and announced, "Boss, I need you to join Baggit full-time!"

We started manufacturing wallets as a new category. I delegated this section entirely to Vishal. My only brief to Vishal was to be creative and design intuitively.

Vicky, who was younger of the two, had joined the company as well. By 1996, I had sent him to train in every department for three months each. He even cut raw material, as I wanted him to learn everything.

The early Baggit team
from the top: Sudhir Mistry, Vicky Ahuja, Nina Lekhi, Vijay Mudaliyar, Sapna Ahuja

A year later, Vicky left Baggit because he had some disagreements with our general manager, Sudhir *bhai*. I had to go to his house and convince him to come back to office. He was not as driven as the rest, but then he was only 18 and he had huge potential. He returned to us after a year. Now, 20 years later, he is Head of Sales and Marketing.

"I used to reach INXS directly after college and sit there till it shut. I learnt everything about retailing in that store. Work was good. I continued till I graduated, soon after which I was married. Two days after my wedding, Nina asked me to work full time at her factory. I was elated. I didn't think even once before saying yes."

—Vishal Ahuja,
Head of Operations, Baggit

I believe I am good at identifying what a person is capable of. For instance, if a team member goes to buy material from China, I can visualize where he might get stuck, what support he will want from the design team or from me. Almost always, my intuition is right.

As an entrepreneur, it is important that I have the

right people working with me. Identifying good people is instinctive, and luckily I possessed this instinct.

> "Nina has great judgment. While she may not visualize at first sight whether someone is a *lambi race ka ghoda,* she can take that person from where they are to where she wants them to be by transmitting her thoughts like a siddha."
>
> *— Mahendra Karkera,*
> *proprietor of Mahesh Lunch Home,*
> *and Nina's best friend*

I began travelling for inspiration and to understand global trends in fashion and design. I visited fashion hubs such as Paris, London and Milan (my favourite!). While I enjoyed the ooh-la-la atmosphere of high-end boutiques, I also loved browsing the street markets. There was something to learn from each one. I was especially eager to understand the product lines, the materials, the cuts being offered, the pricing strategies, and the strengths of international companies similar to Baggit.

While I learned a great deal from international brands, I have never had any reason to copy them. Instead, what worked for me was to focus on gaps in the market in terms of features and material. The products we began churning out in the mid-90s were quite sophisticated. I also ensured that whatever I valued in a bag as a consumer, my customers would experience it in a Baggit bag.

At the same time, I started experimenting with new materials. Leather was big in those days. People thought it was 'pricey.' Customers used to smell products to distinguish original leather from fake.

Until then we hadn't used leather, but one day, ignoring my gut feeling, I brought home a patch of cowhide. I treated and coloured it, and kept it in my verandah overnight to dry. In the morning, the entire house was stinking. I felt terrible and disgusted with what I had done. That's when I decided that I would never ever use leather.

However, I knew customers wanted something that looked and felt like leather. I tried working with synthetic leather. It was a big risk because of the market perception that synthetic was cheap. I kept experimenting with new treatments to get different textures. Eventually, I managed to create the leather finish I desired.

When it came to my designs, I was only satisfied with ideas that were different from what existed in the market. A lot of thought went into them, and I took inputs from everyone. I sought feedback not only from customers, but also from relatives and friends. We would give them sample bags to use, so that they could point out any shortcomings. If their suggestions made sense, I incorporated the changes immediately.

It helped that my sister-in-law, Monica (wife of Manjo's elder brother) is a very detail-oriented person, with an extremely discerning eye. It was she who suggested that every wallet should have several compartments for cards, and be big enough to fit larger currency notes without folding them. Other friends insisted on a zip at the back of wallets and purses in which to keep coins. Customers also suggested design touches such as pockets for glares, contact lenses and makeup – and even a hole for a headphone wire!

I incorporated all such priceless market intelligence into our products. Baggit bags came to be known for their functionality. I would never make a bag conical (narrow-mouthed), simply for the sake of fashion. Baggit products never compromise on practicality for fashion.

For each new product-style, I looked for that one feature that would hook a buyer's attention. The one that would make her automatically buy the bag. It could be an extra pocket for holding a bottle, or a concealed compartment for just-used credit cards, something you always wanted but could never find.

I was uncompromising towards excellence in quality. During the initial years, I bought the best material I could afford and put every product through strict quality control checks at every stage of manufacturing. We had, and continue to have, 100 percent quality inspection of our fabrics, trims, zips and accessories.

My biggest lesson from international products was the support-design aspect. This is the structure with which contents of the bag are held. From the beginning, I was very finicky about the strength of my bags. Every stitch had to be perfect. Customers tell us that our laptop bags do not tear even with the heaviest laptops. This strength is because of the stirrup structure that our bags have. Stirrups are the contraptions used while riding a horse. They bear the rider's feet and support his weight. Similarly, our bags have a strong frame that takes the load and makes them long lasting.

We have always been innovative. Way back in 2001, Baggit was the first company in India to manufacture mobile pouches. Today, most brands have copied this feature. It was Baggit's design team that insisted that a mobile should get its own space in a lady's wallet. If the competition is honest, they will tell you where they saw it first.

Challenges

The first crisis any successful brand faces is imitation. INXS had become popular overnight. We had fraudsters posing as customers, buying samples of our most popular bags and then copying them. Then, we would hear from retailers that someone else was manufacturing our designs for a lower price. We were temporarily placated when we saw the poor quality of the imitations. But something had to be done.

We found new vendors around the world and cemented our rapport with them. We asked them not to sell the materials that we purchased to others, and we ordered custom-made material and purchased it in bulk for a good price.

We got a bigger blow when we discovered that a few of our contract-job workers were moonlighting for the copycats. They were not Baggit employees, but we had invested in training them. We surmounted this issue by hiring supervisors who monitored the contract workers.

Another unexpected issue was gender discrimination among the workers.

I have always aimed to give fair and equal employment to women, but to my dismay, our contractors were paying women less than their male counterparts for the same job. It took me six months to successfully counsel these mostly uneducated men.

Finally, the biggest challenge that we faced between 1989 and 2001 was that of maintaining production during the communal riots in Mumbai after the Babri Mosque demolition on December 6, 1992.

Many of our craftsmen were Muslims, living and working in the communally sensitive areas of Sion, Dharavi and Kurla in Central Mumbai. They were scared to come to work and so were we. Those months which culminated in the bomb blasts of January 1993, in which around 900 people died, were highly stressful. Many of our employees left Mumbai, never to return.

I gave salaries in advance to those who wished to work. Our employees' fear of coming to work was justified and, as an exception, I allowed them to take material home. I also assured them that they could come back, whenever they felt safe, with the finished products. They were so heart-warmingly sincere; they kept sending finished goods whenever they could.

LEARNING:

Focus on work, not its rewards.

I have fumed at seeing my original designs copied. I wanted to scream at these copycats in person and prove to them that they were cheats, but I couldn't stop them. As the *Bhagwad Gita* says, *"Karmanye Vadhikaraste Ma Phaleshu Kadachana"* (You only have the right to work, but not to its fruits). I stopped thinking about them, as work was consuming all my waking hours – and the numbers on Baggit's balance sheet reminded me that 'honest work always pays'. For the second time in my life, my belief in hard work was QED- *Quod erat demonstrandum* (hence proven).

4

The Biggest Milestone of My Life

Even after marriage, Baggit had all my attention. Moving into Manjo's home did not change my lifestyle at all. I clearly had the coolest in-laws in the world! They loved me even more than my parents did. Have you heard of a Punjabi man who offers his daughter-in-law a pack of cigarettes?

I am not making this up. My father-in-law has never once told me, "*Kudi, ek cup chai bana ke laa* (get me a cuppa, girl)!" Nor has Manjo's mother ever told me to cook dinner for the family. Compared to how most young girls are treated in their husbands' homes, I have had a fairy-tale marriage.

I think this love has made a tremendous contribution to my success.

In fact, Manjo's mother is a sweet, cuddly ball of love.

She had a very tough life when her own mother-in-law was around. Instead of passing the frustration forward, she became the ideal, supportive mother-in-law to us. By doing this, she let go of her own pain – and also won my unconditional affection forever.

> *"Shuru main humein tension tha, ki Sindhi ladkiyaan itni hi-fi hoti hai, humare ghar main adjust hogi kya? Lekin Nina ne mere apno se badkar mera khayaal rakha hai."*
>
> (Initially, we were tense because Sindhi girls were known to be quite hi-fi, so we were worried whether Nina would adjust in our home. But she has taken care of me more than my own family.)"
>
> ***— Mrs. Ved Lekhi,***
> ***Nina's mother-in-Law***

On the other hand, my relationship with Rita took a slight turn for the worse. Rita's status had now changed from best friend to sister-in-law. Little things such as her wiping her lipstick on my towel, which wouldn't have bothered me before, were now beginning to irritate me. She was also feeling the strain of the new relationship – of our being together constantly.

In the first year of our marriage, Manjo and I behaved

Nina with her mother-in-law, Ved

as if we were still in college. However, we were beginning to get tired of pub hopping. How many times can you drink, throw up and come home? It was a habit and we didn't know how to break it. We knew no other way of entertaining ourselves.

One major concern at home was that my mother-in-law was suffering from serious insomnia. Medicines had not worked. I saw her struggle without sleep through many nights and I mentioned this to my mother. She suggested that we immediately take Manjo's mother for a meditation program called Siddha Samadhi Yoga (SSY).

So it was that the four of us – Manjo, Rita, my mom-in-law and me – enrolled for a 15-day SSY workshop in November of 1989. Actually, the three of us tagged along only to give mom some company.

This workshop required us to reach the venue on an empty stomach at six in the morning. To get there on time, we had to wake up at 5 am, which was completely unheard of for Manjo and me – we were used to going to sleep at that time.

When I first heard of the timing, I did this drama of pushing an imaginary knife deep into my heart, screaming 'Kill me instead!' It seemed easier to die than wake up at five. What was worse was that the minute we entered the class, the teacher made us sit in Vajrasana pose, which requires that one place one's entire body weight on the calves and heels while keeping the spine erect. Ouch!

On the first day of the workshop itself, we experienced a miracle. All three of us – Manjo, Rita and I – were fast asleep in Vajrasana with absolutely erect backs. The teacher had to call our names every ten minutes to wake us up!

Every day, for the next 15 days, we experienced the power of improved lung capacity due to deeply-energizing breathing exercises and a raw diet. We were taught to challenge our past negative beliefs and to transcend petty thinking. The course also took us to a higher level of composure with practical philosophies to handle daily stress.

And, to our collective amazement, my mother-in-law was cured of her years of insomnia within one fortnight. We were all impressed. This workshop was like nothing we had experienced before – and it completely changed our way of thinking.

We were drawn into the SSY culture. We became aware that, normally, our minds are either occupied in thinking of the past or the future. Now, we were taught to enjoy the present moment. This realization set us free of debilitating thoughts, memories and guilt. We also experienced the culture of silence. What a powerful and life-altering technique it was to be able to silence the ever chattering mind.

The course also led Manjo to realize how disillusioned he was with our current lifestyle. He was drawn to every aspect of the program. He listened ardently to Guruji and was keen to follow all instructions to a T.

"We were fortunate that, when we completed the SSY program, we were initiated in the presence of Guruji himself. Like any new student, I had so many questions about our constant struggles to be happy in the material world. Guruji never answered questions. He told me, 'You be with me for two years, and come for the advanced meditation courses'. Both Nina and I committed to visit the ashram six times a year for our inner growth."

— Manoj Lekhi,
Nina's husband

Our Guruji suggested that we remain in touch with SSY teachings by enrolling for the advanced workshops. Initially, Manjo went to the ashram for a short stay every two months, but slowly his involvement increased. A year later, both of us went for the teachers' training course at Ahobilam, Andhra Pradesh. It was a 180-degree change for both of us, inside out.

Manjo was blown away by the way his thought process had transformed. Both of us became more mindful and started connecting deeply with others. We also experienced an immense lightness of being, as we were following the ashram diet and meditating three times a day.

Rita and I also resolved our petty issues and became close again. We had become calmer within. Everyone at home noticed the change.

During our SSY classes, Guruji had told us to meditate even in the afternoon. This was damn tough at work. I noticed Manjo getting more and more disinclined to come to the office. When he did come to the office, he made it a point to find a place where we could meditate without being disturbed or judged by others.

In those days, our Lalbaug factory did not have bathrooms in every *gala*. There was just one shared washroom at the end of the corridor.

Since the industrial estate was not fully occupied, the bathroom on our floor mostly remained locked and was pretty clean, so we used to take the key, as entitled *gala* owners, open the bathroom, and meditate inside.

Sometimes we found a place behind piles of fabric to meditate. We couldn't meditate in front of others because people did not understand what we were doing. Nor could we explain to everyone. We were a bit self-conscious ourselves, initially. I was amazed to witness how much Manjo was changing.

I must recount a significant incident that happened just before our wedding. Manjo, my boyfriend at the time, said, "If I ask you right now to leave your business for me, would you leave it?"

I replied, "Yes."

The question was strange and very unlike him. He was testing me, just as women are tested every day, everywhere around the globe – forced to make choices that will make us look good when viewed from others' lenses, and perhaps even our own lenses once we become mothers. We are expected to choose work only with the approval of patriarchs and always be a step behind them.

Manjo did not really want me to leave my business but he was your typical possessive North Indian man until SSY happened to him.

But I was not able to surrender myself to the SSY culture the way he did. My business was picking up and

> "I had some terrible habits before I was introduced to SSY. My behaviour was clearly that of a possessive, Punjabi male. It was my conditioning, my limited beliefs, that my wife Nina should be dedicated only to me. We have hundreds of friends in our group – and I literally used to experience this physical burning in my chest if she went to the disco with other boys.

Slowly, by being with Guruji, attending all the courses, I began to realize how wrong I was, and that I could change only myself – that the way to my freedom was through intellectual understanding. I understood that the truth behind my nagging was that there was something incomplete within me, and I was determined to sort myself out. Else, controlling her would have eventually led to her controlling me. Yes, initially she would have listened under pressure, but surely resented me later.

The main realization was: Who the hell was I to stop her? Both of us were different human beings, and here (on earth) together for some time. In the end, she would go, and so would I. What will we gain by controlling each other? There was something more attractive for us to seek: the knowledge of the next level. And in that quest of that higher truth, I attended this program called SSY-BST (Bhaava Samaadhi Training). All the answers came naturally to me from within. I didn't need to struggle or ask Guruji any more questions."

— Manoj Lekhi,
Nina's husband

required a lot of my energy. Manjo wanted less of the material world and more of the bliss that SSY offered.

He felt it was his calling to walk down the spiritual path. I tried to resist his detachment from the material life for seven years – until 1997.

Unable to handle it, I often drove from the office to Worli Sea Face, just to cry alone. I sobbed as I imagined Manjo with a long *daadhi* and *lungi* looking like a Sadhu-baba. Everyone was struggling with this change in him, but we could not stop him.

By 1997, Manjo decided to leave his business completely. It came as a rude shock to his family, especially to his brother, Sunil, with whom Manjo had started Zedd's. Manjo said that he no longer wanted to work in the business. For Sunil, this was a very big change because Manjo had always looked after Zedd's finance, accounts and purchase departments. I recall one particular instance, just after Manjo quit, when there was an income tax enquiry at Zedd's. Nobody could reach Manjo, as he was travelling all over the country for his workshops. There were no cell phones then.

Slowly, over time, they learned to manage without him; there was no choice.

I was devastated, but I didn't stop him. After having attended the same courses, I understood why he wanted to go down that road so much.

A lot of factors helped me to accept Manjo's transition.

"Nina completely changed after SSY. She was unconditionally in love with Manjo and she lost a lot of her flamboyance. They always wanted to be with each other but after SSY, the possessiveness and bondage vanished. She is a businesswoman and he a spiritual guru. Both walk their own path with complete freedom. When I see them together, I realize how evolved they are."

— Rita Lekhi,
Nina's childhood friend and sister-in-law

First of all, I had a spiritual foundation at home. My mother used to be deeply involved in *satsangs* when I was young, and there was no resentment towards this from my father. Sure, her absence was tough for him, but he never stood in her way. For us kids, dad was our role model, and we imbibed his acceptance. I realized that one couldn't fight the inevitable or force anyone to stay away from what they truly want to do. This helped me to be supportive of Manjo.

Additionally, my in-laws were calm and loving. The way Manjo and Sunil separated from the business after we left their parents' home in 2000 was very peaceful, compared to what usually happens.

It was because Manjo went so deep into SSY that I

attended all the advanced meditation workshops with him.

"Nina adjusted with my surrender into the spiritual world because she had witnessed the magic of SSY herself. She knew the context, and the reason for my turnaround. The only difference was that she did not turn around to the extent that I did, and that was her choice. But she was always supportive and I am deeply grateful to her for that. If she were not part of this whole transformation, we would have definitely gone our own ways, or be like many couples: stuck together but cursing one another from inside."

— Manoj Lekhi,
Nina's husband

If Manjo had not dedicated his life to spreading the messages of SSY, I don't think I would be involved with the ashram to such a great extent. Not only that, I probably wouldn't be involved with my mom's or anyone else's spiritual group. This may be because I am not spiritual in the typical sense. What I call spirituality is a feeling of loving and sharing what you have with others.

I recall being generous even as a child, but during the

years when I was dating Manjo, I experienced a higher level of sharing and generosity.

Our significantly large gang of nine would hang around at Manjo's home five days a week. Theirs was a typical Punjabi house where food and drinks kept flowing, until each and every one of us had left. Not once during all of our get-togethers did I ever hear Manjo's mom say, "Why do all of you party only at our house?" She was always smiling radiantly when she welcomed us. She loved that the kids were partying at her home.

Those years were proof of the 'Lekhi large-heartedness,' as Manjo's father was in deep debt then. He was managing the family business and they had taken numerous loans to stay afloat through lean business cycles. While their turnover was in crores, the terms that he had borrowed on were designed to keep him in debt. He lost most of his revenues in litigation.

At the Lekhi residence, however, no one ever counted how much was spent when people were together. They prioritized generosity and joy over stress and sorrow. None of their children (or their friends) ever felt debt-ridden.

My marriage into this extraordinary family taught me that relationships are most important. It is unnecessary to obsessively think of money, because there is always enough for all. And this attitude of sharing has worked for my business as well.

LEARNING:
Vidya and Avidya.

SSY encourages you to be selfish about knowledge of the self (Vidya), but selfless about knowledge of the outside or the material world (Avidya). Manjo inspired me to start incorporating all SSY teachings into my business. I encouraged my staff to attend SSY programs in order to personally understand the concepts that were benefiting us. I was inspired to give back to the communities that had indirectly or directly helped Baggit grow. We inaugurated personality and computer classes for children, as well as education for parents in nearby villages. This led to a spiritual revolution for Baggit and every employee that would work with us. Little did we know that the goal of creating harmony for our stakeholders would get us unimaginable rewards.

5

CEO-Mom is Not an Oxymoron

In the year 1999, two years after Manjo joined SSY full-time, we began the search for our own home. Almost immediately, we zeroed in on a particular apartment and moved in. Our new home had such positive vibrations that within the first month of moving in, after twelve years of marriage, I conceived. We had been trying to have a baby for almost ten long years.

The timing of what happened has been divine. We became parents only when we were sure of our calling in life. We were ready to focus on nurturing a baby. But there was a lesson I learned even while buying this apartment, which I want to share.

We were four families living in the three-bedroom Lekhi home. Even though the relationships were harmonious, the space crunch prompted the move. One of the first apartments we looked at was a tiny one in Shivaji Park, on the topmost floor of a building. It had no lift. The USP of this building was its unrestricted view of the sea. Both Manjo and I were used to this since childhood. When we saw the flat, I hated it! But Manjo thought it was out of this world. I was taken aback. I could not fathom what it was that impressed him so much. It was also Ganesh Chaturthi that day, and we were deafened by sounds of the *dhol,* being played by a huge crowd downstairs. Secondly, the house was a one-bedroom hall kitchen, which had been remoulded into eight tiny turquoise-colored rooms. Even the terrace was falling apart.

"My mom is an all-rounder! She is good at swimming, cooking and business. She designs cool printed bags with great zips. My friends say mom can do anything and everything for me – and that she is a great inspiration to everyone. The best part about her is that she never takes any decision about anybody (including me and my friends) without consulting his or her opinion. According to me, that's her best quality."

— Vedoci Lekhi,
Nina's daughter

Manjo's mom rightly called it a *chidia ghar.* She kept mumbling, 'so dirty' to herself. She was most displeased about the missing lift. Of course, the broker said, "This year they will install the lift, don't worry." (It's been 17 years and there is still no lift!)

Manjo, as always, had an extraordinarily different perspective. He was hell-bent on buying it – and we did. We then got the entire house redesigned by our friends Chandan and Ritesh, who turned it around into a gorgeous open space. They remoulded it to look like a residential spa.

I was blown away when I saw the ready flat. The entrance opened up into a spacious open-air lounge. In one cosy corner, lounge chairs and a glass table had been placed. The east-facing wall held a huge portrait of our Guruji, Shree Rishi Prabhakar. The space around his image exuded calm, with several niches holding lamps and Ganesha and Buddha idols. Creepers garlanded these idols, taking roots on the rustic tiles. Adjacent to the lounge was my open kitchen, where I baked before chilling either in the living room or bedroom.

Opposite to the main entrance, Chandan created a spiral staircase taking us to our own private terrace. Here, we beheld a panoramic view of the Arabian Sea. Manjo and I demarcated this area for meditation, and planned to hold SSY workshops there.

Lastly, the new interiors were completely baby-friendly. Who would have known that an ordinary looking apartment on the top of a building would make us feel like we were on top of the world!

On May 6, 2000, our daughter, Vedoci, was born. Suddenly, an adorable baby kicked awry my sales target, reporting and design schedules.

I found the experience of motherhood beautiful, but extremely overwhelming. Vedoci came along less than a year after we took the bold step of living in a nuclear family. And I found the routine of managing the baby all day long to be quite monotonous.

Maybe that is why I was anxious to get back to work within three months of giving birth to Vedoci.

But every day, like all new mothers, I could never predict what time I would actually manage to leave home. The baby's feeding and napping schedule was unpredictable. It completely changed the way I perceived the female staff in my organization. My own experience as a mother made me deeply empathetic.

Manjo was now regularly conducting SSY training programs on his own and this kept him busy in the evenings. I tried reorganizing work hours to leave early and reach home before he left, but he was often traveling or had all-day training programs. Those days, I had to stay put at home.

It was okay to work from home for a day or two every week but, beyond that, I had to go to the office.

Nina with her daughter, Vedoci

How many times could I call everyone home? Besides, it was really boring to sit at home. I was fed up with having only maids for company. I felt withdrawal pangs. I needed to do something creative. I looked around for encouragement and ideas.

How did other working mothers manage?

Inspiration arrived from the most unexpected quarter. An image I'd seen a thousand times before suddenly struck me as the coolest idea ever: the *chaddar-ka-jhula* tied to trees to support construction workers. What a brilliant invention to carry little babies to work!

The very next day, I took Vedoci to office. I hung a bed sheet in my cabin with an attached string to swing it! Whenever Vedo cried, I fed her on demand. It was like working at home. If I needed to step out, I just carried her with me. I guess I was able to do it because it was my own company. Both baby and mummy were at peace and I could still give full attention to the business.

Suddenly, I was raring to go!

It was just as well, as there soon came a phase, before the end of the year 2000, when Baggit faced a huge challenge as part of the Indian bag industry. The Indian market was witnessing a sudden influx of 'Made in China' bags. This badly hit our sales volumes.

I could not reduce the prices of existing products because they were reasonable in terms of their cost. It was not long before my oldest and friendliest buyer, Shopper's

Stop, asked me to help them wage war with these Chinese imports. I felt honoured and excited to design a couple of bags priced ₹899 and ₹999, which they purchased in bulk. I used a new, inexpensive, durable and lightweight material to make these bags. Needless to say, the low price, coupled with high Baggit quality and functionality, led to high-volume sales. I suddenly felt back in form, and was happy playing supermom to my *bada* baby, Baggit, along with my new *chhota* baby, Vedoci.

The year 2000 was a special year for me.

Our annual sale at INXS was held in November 2000. We were still doing everything ourselves. Post 8 pm, I strapped in seven-month-old Vedoci and drove her to the store. When we arrived, every square foot of INXS was covered with cartons and merchandise. There was no place to keep her. Suddenly, I noticed that the window display was filled with balloons, but otherwise unused. I cleared it out and placed my baby in the window display section. Can you imagine a seven-month-old sleeping in the window display behind the glass? I'm sure passers-by must have rubbed their eyes in amazement.

Mukesh and I set up the store until 10 pm, and Vedo, as the saying goes, slept through it like a baby!

Another huge struggle for me was my post-pregnancy weight. I love being fit, and was paranoid about the weight I'd gained. Like any new mom, I found it futile even to try going for a jog. Not that I didn't give it a shot, but someone always called me back home to sooth the wailing Vedo within 15 minutes. Still, I joined a gym because I was hell-bent on working out. I chose one that had a dance room where I could take the baby along. I would keep Vedo with her toys on one side and exercise or dance around with a trainer nearby. It was like play for her to see me jump around.

Before we knew it, she started going to playschool. For a few months, she just slept in the car after playschool. Slowly, however, her need for an afternoon nap also disappeared. I remember telling my driver and maid to keep driving around until she fell asleep. They called me after two hours to say it hadn't worked.

Even before Vedoci was five and could express how she felt, I realized she did not want to go to somebody else's house. She wanted her own space to play, so I began calling my dad or my mom-in-law for help. They were very supportive during this phase, and were available at my beck and call. Our lift-less residence was a pain for my mom-in-law, but she would willingly climb four floors just to be with Vedo. I feel very blessed that they supported us like this but, understandably, I couldn't call them every day.

I worked a lot from home to adapt to the changing needs of my child, rather than making her adapt to my timings. Soon, I was blessed with Amma, a loving caretaker for Vedoci who appeared like magic in my life when I needed her the most. Amma is the mother of Vijay Mudaliyar – the absolutely indispensable Head of Production at Baggit. Vijay single-handedly manages our 250-person labor department. Besides keeping me worry-free when it comes to factory labour issues, he also rescued me when I was unable to find trusted help to manage Vedo. Vijay convinced his adorable mother to help me out. It was a favour I can never repay because, except for working at my home until Vedoci was older, Amma worked nowhere else. She stayed with me 24/7 and took care of Vedoci's every need until I got home. She has unconditional affection for Vedoci, which we see till date.

Soon, Vedoci started demanding more from me. "Mom, come to school to fetch me! All the other mothers come; why don't you?" I used to explain to her that the other mothers weren't running a business. Several mothers were actually attending kitty parties in the afternoons.

I explained to Vedoci that businesses cannot be neglected. As a Managing Director, I cannot afford to be absent. I made sure I always made it for an important event, but the daily grind of dropping and fetching her was tough.

Being the MD doesn't make you immune to mommy guilt. After Vedoci's demands began, I did *s*tretch myself. I made it to school every day.

I don't want to imply that women can't have it all – nothing in life is black and white.

For most men, getting back home really late at night is acceptable; however, most women are DNA-programmed to make themselves sick with guilt if they haven't spent time with their child. Knowing that their child is with paid help keeps them on tenterhooks. Their imagination also runs wild, fearing neglect or mischief.

Work has a part-time role in a woman's life and sense of achievement, so there is no point comparing ourselves to men. We should be elated that we are different and have an excess of that cuddly motherhood hormone: oxytocin.

I think women are the lucky ones. For instance, if I have to do a press interview, I do it at home without any qualms. I can honestly tell them that, as a mother, I am constantly multitasking. Mothers are privileged to have the ability to give and nurture life. You should not let anyone make you feel sorry that you need to get back to your little one. If you feel confident and proud to be a mother, people will read your body language and treat you the way you feel inside.

In the office too, if a man comes late *chaar baar*, my HR nags him; but if a woman comes in late, the same people (at least at Baggit, and I'm sure in a lot of other places as well) gently inquire whether she is having some issue at home. This, however, is unusual. As a patriarchal nation we generally have little empathy for the working woman. There should be more empathy and respect for her.

At Baggit, I have consciously hired more women,

even as office peons. There are no uniform-clad boys in my office. My sari-clad angels do it all – whether it is photocopying, serving pre-lunch salad or tea, or even packing cartons.

And it's not just me. The world around us is changing, though not at the desired pace. As Bob Dylan said, 'the times, they are a-changin'. Today, many men support their wives at work and honestly admit that a lot of the women they have met are way smarter than they are. Many homes are now thriving on double incomes, with men pitching in with the housework. Even women who don't have careers spend their lives caring for the family unit, which is the backbone of the work force.

When Manjo, whom I regard as the ideal man, conducts relationship workshops, he makes funny references to how men are. If they are watching TV, they are doing just that single task. But when a woman watches TV, she also talks to the *istriwala* at the door and has an eye on the kids. Of course men also do this, but in most cases this is after thorough training by his lady.

This kind of multi-tasking is essential to doing well in business. You can't sit in one meeting and say that you forgot to follow up on something else. Manjo says that women have better business sense. Even as Managing Director, I think women are better at everything.

Challenges

A business challenge, which came up the same year that Vedoci was born, baffled me more than the miracles of motherhood.

As I was approaching my delivery date, the scattered *galas* at Narayan Udyog Bhavan became difficult to navigate. I felt it was time to have my entire team in one place, rather than spread over three floors at the industrial estate. Baggit was also quickly growing and all the teams felt it made sense to move, so we took a comparatively huge 15,000 square feet premises on rent.

Within a few months of the shift, business declined. In the history of Baggit, it was the first time that our products were not selling well. Large orders were abruptly cancelled. There were challenges with raising working capital. Overheads shot up and we could not understand why – we were not doing anything different. In spite of speaking to the old, loyal buyers, we could not surmount the issues that cropped up.

I used to complain about this to trusted friends, when one of them suggested we consult a *Vaastu* expert. None of us at Baggit believed in *Vaastu*, but since there was no other solution in sight, we agreed to consult an expert out of curiosity.

The minute the consultant walked into our new office,

he said, "Boss, there is a problem here. The entry is wrong, all the energy you are putting into this premises is getting lost." He ominously predicted that things would continue to worsen if we did not shift. We were reluctant to move because, if we did, the lease agreement for the premise required us to pay for the locked-in period of two years. Besides, the entire experience had already been very troublesome. We had spent a lot on renovation of the new place; but business was getting worse by the minute.

We felt it would be better to move again, but we had burned our fingers and, after everything, we didn't feel comfortable shifting to a new place. The Baggit team, including me, felt safe returning only to Narayan Udyog Bhavan.

To make matters worse, when we inquired about the *galas* that we had previously rented, only two of the six were available. The rest had been rented to others. Still, we did a *ghar-vaapsi*. Incredibly, as soon we returned, the business immediately started flourishing like magic. As a result, all of us now believe in *Vaastu*. For any new property, we wait until our *Vaastu* consultant gives it a thumbs-up.

LEARNING:

Tune into your intelligence.

Managing a newborn is really tough, but most new parents do it instinctively, without any training. I was persistent enough to juggle work, care for my baby and focus on my exercise routine – even though it often felt impossible to manage everything together. I did not pull myself down by saying negative things like 'I can't do this anymore.' Similarly, I have never said to myself, 'I hate numbers,' or 'I can't read long reports'. As my organization grew, I learned a lot of complex theories on the job by tuning into my innate intelligence. This survival skill can take us through the toughest phases of business as well. Yes, there will be moments when you want to give up. When that happens, closing your eyes and sitting in silence will bring you the most creative solutions to problems. Like the *chaddar* swing.

6

Large-Format Stores and a Large-Format Life

Phase 3 of Baggit: 2001-2006

While I was grappling with these huge changes in my personal life, the bag and luggage industry in India was also witnessing a sea change.

We had a particular style of working with department stores such as Amarson's and Shopper's Stop, which had been buying from us monthly since 1991. They gave us orders, paid us, and we dispatched the stock.

I was in love with Shopper's Stop and wanted to work with them since the day they opened their doors in Mumbai. Shopper's had always played safe with us. Their contract had a clause that allowed them to return unsold stock to us. I allowed this because while I could easily liquidate stock in a sale, I did not want them to reduce their budget for new purchases. And it turned out to be a good decision, because while returns happened only once or twice in ten years, they gave us awesome sales every month.

In the year 2001, the Indian retail market came into its own. The country's first hypermarket concept, Future Group's Big Bazaar opened at High Street Phoenix, Lower Parel. Before that, Piramal's Crossroads had opened in Mahalakshmi but had failed to get much traction. These LFSs (large-format stores) were revolutionizing the retail business.

Pantaloons (also owned by Future Group) was the first to tell us, "Boss, we can't buy your stock outright. We will give you space with your own branding for you to place your stock on credit. On the basis of whatever sells, we'll give you a share of the money."

This was called the 'sale-or-return' (SOR) model, which was new to us. It was so damn weird. We thought, *yaar*, we've never worked like this. I had a block in my mind that if they were not paying then they would not take care of our stock either; that they'd return damaged stock saying it didn't sell. This made us feel very vulnerable. I had always thought of my bags as my babies and I did not feel like sending them off alone, without a caretaker.

But entrepreneurship means venturing into the unknown. I had constantly taken leaps of faith, but now I could ask for my own terms. I said, "Ok, Baggit will use your space; but we want our own person standing at the counter to deal with customers." They readily agreed.

There was an enthusiastic boy working with us. I told

"Nina's vision was to make the brand big. I have seen that time where buyers (retail) were like gods for us. They would suddenly buy Chinese or imported stock and abruptly tell us, 'No *yaar*, we don't have an OTB (open-to-buy) budget this month as we are overstocked.' And we would be in no position to argue. But with shop-in-shops, the shift was that Baggit would get a dedicated space and customers would demand our brand. The brand became as popular as the retailer."

— Vicky Ahuja,
Head of Sales & Marketing, Baggit

him, "Boss, we will give you growth; but you have to stand at our counter in Pantaloons and sell the best you can!" He was super excited. We offered him a commission for each piece he sold, and he ensured fabulous sales.

Soon after we started SOR with Pantaloons, another well-known store called Sayonara on Linking Road wanted to stock our bags.

In 2005, I was voted one of the '50 Most Powerful

Businesswomen in India' by *Business Today*. This was my adrenaline shot. It amplified the recognition we were already getting.

By next year, I had enough confidence to open Baggit's first EBO (exclusive brand outlet) at the Atria (Millennium) Mall in Worli, Mumbai. Initially, I didn't think this new mall would do well. Having lived in Worli for the longest time, I felt the location of the mall as well as its car park was pretty inconvenient.

> "Sayonara was retailing imitation jewelry. Its owner admittedly didn't know the business of bags, but promised us premium space. And Nina asked him for the world. She told him, 'I want Baggit branding outside and inside the store, I will keep bags only at the premium space on the ground floor.' The sweet fellow agreed to all our terms. We sold rupees four to five lakh worth of bags in the first month. The owner was elated and so were we."
>
> *–Sapna Karkera-Ahuja, former Head of Marketing, Baggit*

By then I had attended a program called 'Professional Insights,' conducted by Manjo, and he motivated me to create a future by being totally focused on my vision. My vision at the time was to break into retail. I felt the time had come to launch Baggit's own Exclusive Brand Outlet. I could have rented a store in a new mall in Malad too, but that was a two-hour drive from home. Choosing a distant location for my EBO would have left me unable to care for my baby the way I wished to – so Atria it was.

At the time, Vicky felt that we should start with something we could afford. He believed that in a store, at best, our sales would be 2-3 lakh. So he went to Atria and selected a small store on the second floor because the rentals for shops on the ground floor were sky-high.

I felt, however, that our first store should be at a premium location, so I insisted on a ground floor store, diagonally opposite the international luxury lingerie brand La Senza.

Sixteen years after I stained my clothes painting our first shop with Mukesh, we hired a high-profile interior designer (who had designed stores for Regal and Inc5) to design our store from scratch. He selected the colours white and brown for our store. My heart swelled with pride, knowing that this store was the first of many. All of them would have the same brand identity.

Soon, I realized that Vicky had been right. The rent was exorbitant. It was ₹2,90,000 per month, and though the store gave us good sales of ₹3,00,000, it was just enough to cover the rent. Overheads such as electricity

Baggit store at Atria

and cost of raw material were paid out of pocket.

Even so, I still think of my decision to start a store at Atria as magical, because it created a lot of awareness in Mumbai about Baggit as a brand. Franchisees started calling us to open stores for us.

What a turning point it was!

Challenges: Lag in Production

With all these SOR counters in malls, demand for our products skyrocketed. To meet the requirement, we increased the number of workers in every unit. We also started cutting our material in-house to expedite the process and sent the pieces to job-working setups. Once stitched, the ready products were sent back to our factory.

Before these large-format stores appeared, we were paying our workers per piece, 45 days after receiving finished goods. Now, not only were we able to pay for any machinery required by them, we also cleared their dues within a week's time; however, we were still unable to meet the demand.

I investigated to find out what the real problem was. That's when I learned that our job-workers preferred work with three basic elements: consistency, timely payments (including credit facility), and a good wage.

I knew I could not scale up unless the people who worked for me were happy. Manjo was my in-house reminder of these SSY philosophies, so I instructed my team to make it a point to meet *all* the needs of my workers. We changed our terms so that we were, and still are, the best paymasters in our industry.

To make sure that the ecosystem of vendors and job-workers were happy too, I thought backwards. I realized that the only foolproof method to ensure that workers' payments were made in the desired time frame was to include this into the KRAs (Key Result Areas) of my accounts department. This meant that if they were not paid on time, it would be the accounts department that would suffer and not my worker.

It worked beautifully; the paymasters never delayed a payment again. My finance team rightly pointed out that my decision denied us credit period advantages enjoyed by others, but in my opinion, this decision worked to Baggit's overall advantage. We created bonds of trust with the workers forever.

Another challenge in the year 2006 was the formation of unions by a few workers who made demands such as sick leave and provident fund. Though these benefits were not available for contract workers, we were already proactively working on offering other benefits. When we spoke to them, we realized that they were not disgruntled *only* about this. There were more fundamental issues.

One entire worker unit doubted their prospects working for an organization led by a woman. These people quit soon, and I did not stop them. I find it easier to train new people than deal with negativity. These very people who doubted the potential of Baggit in the 90s are now stunned by our growth.

LEARNING:

Vairagya or detachment towards wealth leads to more of it.

I can make these bold decisions of doing away with credit advantages because I have consciously incorporated spiritual thinking into my business. Guruji explained to us that money, or Goddess Lakshmi, is just a form of energy. This energy is neutral, ever flowing, and needs to be exchanged to create more of it. It is true that we are not used to the concept of giving away in business. But by practicing silence, I have achieved detachment towards wealth. This came easily to me as I have never been truly attached to money. Yes, I want to see Baggit become an internationally-acclaimed brand, but I'm not obsessed with collecting or hoarding wealth at a personal level. I've always been a giver; I spend generously (not casually) wherever it is warranted. This has always opened new channels to grow and create beautiful services for all.

7

My Three-Day Workweek

As Baggit hurriedly grew bigger, so did Vedoci. Sometimes, I wondered if they were trying to keep pace with each other.

Though Manjo and I were busy, we were absolutely hands-on as parents. Manjo was not happy with the teaching methodology in schools where we were seeking admission for Vedoci. There was too much emphasis on theoretical learning and very little on experiential learning.

In 2001, when Vedoci was a year old, Manjo, along with Mr. Sunil Karve of Mumbai Educational Trust (MET), jointly launched a school based on SSY teachings. The trustees were aware of the SSY culture and were keen to invest in the idea.

This new school was called Rishikul Vidyalaya, and

was located in Bandra. In its first academic year, the school had only 14 students.

As the director of the school, Manjo encouraged parents to get actively involved in the education of their child. Positive word-of-mouth publicity from happy parents led to another 90 admissions by the second academic year.

> "What impressed me the most was that the children were allowed to learn from experiences. One of the big highlights of the school was that learning was only by play, using ISP techniques such as flashcards, pictures and songs. Children were directly taught sentences. By the age of four, most of the kids could read newspapers."
>
> *– Narendra Anantrane,*
> *parent of a former student at*
> *MET's Rishikul Vidyalaya*

What made the school a total win-win in my eyes was that the structured ICSE board was complemented by an innovative holistic education system. Besides academics, children were trained in classical instruments such as the *tabla,* the *dholak* and the flute. There were meditation sessions daily, and sports such as karate and skating were taught within school hours. Children were encouraged to attempt all activities and pursue what they felt comfortable with. As a result, Vedoci learned to play many musical instruments.

Thanks to these in-house extra-curricular activities, I did not have to coordinate after-school activities like other parents; but every Saturday, I visited the school to attend the mandatory SSY classes on effective parenting. Manjo had made this mandatory for all parents and I was no exception.

The school focused on the concept of yogic *prana* or life-force. Every day one parent was requested to bring freshly cooked *sattvik*, healthy lunch for all students. This ensured that the food served to the kids was nutritious and made with love. It also helped the children develop a taste for a variety of cuisines.

Less than seven years later, in 2008, the Rishi Samskruti Vidya Kendra (RSVK) school management committee developed differences with the Mumbai Educational Trust (MET). Manjo would have wanted to continue managing this school, but the doors of MET had closed for good.

I was left with no option but to scout for another school for Vedoci in the city.

Little did I know that, once again, something totally unexpected would be asked of me.

At the same time that I was looking for a good school, Guruji was keen to start a residential school within the ashram at Katarkhadak. He believed in the idea of a residential school, as he wanted to teach children to spend their evenings doing things other than playing with electronic gadgets or sitting in front of the TV.

"Around 2007, Nina and I attended a Bhava Samadhi workshop conducted by Guruji, where he inspired us to think beyond Mumbai and attempt living in rural India with a like-minded community. A few months later, Nina and I had gone to see two huge plots of land at Katarkhadak. Out of the blue, Guruji told us to set up an SSY ashram there. It was so barren and deserted that Nina angrily told me, 'I want nothing to do with this place!' Hilariously, life soon taught us the true meaning of 'never say never'!"

– Manoj Lekhi,
Nina's husband

Guruji soon asked Manjo to build the RSVK's residential school and ashram from scratch at a huge plot of land in Katarkhadak! This was at a distance of about 180 kms from Mumbai, near Hinjewadi in Pune. It was an unused plot of 150 acres, which had been jointly purchased by Pune's SSY meditators in 1998.

Manjo was also taken aback when he saw how desolate this plot was. There was not even a *pukka* road leading up to the plot. It was a 45-minute climb every time we wanted to see it.

But Manjo could not refuse Guruji's request. He agreed to set up the school and the ashram, even though we had never done anything like this before.

Manjo then told me that he had to 'walk the talk' by enrolling Vedoci.

I could not digest this. It was very tough for me because it meant that my only child would be away from me, and not in Mumbai, for the entire academic year.

I could not refuse Manjo, but my strings were tied to Mumbai because of Baggit. I felt so lost and confused. I had no intention of spending weeks without seeing my family, but I did not know how to manage my business without physically being at the office every day.

After much self-convincing, I embraced this huge change, which at the time I was sure would ruin my life; but, like all the times when I have listened to Manjo, this turned out to be another extraordinary experience.

Manjo has never forced me to do anything. Setting up the school at Katarkhadak was challenging for him too; but he did it because of his complete surrender to Guruji and his obliviousness to his own needs in comparison. He had a valid concern that if, as a parent, he did not send his own child to the new school, it would appear as if he did not believe in it.

It is true that it was a risk to send Vedo to a residential school out of the city. But it was a calculated risk, because Manjo would be involved with the school. The fact that he is a doting parent and excellent with children is well known. I knew his optimism would rub off on me, and that he would leave no stone unturned in setting up the most child-friendly school in Maharashtra.

So, with his friend Kapil, Manjo began making presentations of the upcoming school to old and new SSY meditators all over India. They also tried to convince the parents who had enrolled their children to *Rishikul Vidyalaya* (Bandra), but only six sets of parents committed to send their wards to the new school. Among them, four couples were close friends. They are Kapil and Bindu, Narendra and Varsha, Durgesh and Leena, and Jayshree and Hiten. They were really the core team who did whatever was humanly possible to get the school on track.

Approximately 250 SSY meditators, who had experienced the change within, came to Katarkhadak to assess the offer. Of these, only 30 gutsy parents committed to enrolling their kids in the school. That is why the new residential school was referred to as a school of 'extraordinary parents.' It was they who had to take the leap of faith.

The SSY way of life was so powerful that, before

academic year one had begun, even before a single cottage was constructed, 36 children were admitted to the school.

The USP of the new school was its pedagogy. For instance, to teach first standard students about Punjab, teachers demonstrated a Punjabi song and dance sequence in Punjabi attire. Then the children were given Punjabi food to taste. Only after all this were they shown where Punjab was on the map. Theory was always preceded by activities that piqued the child's interest.

Even Maths, which I feared as a kid, was taught via the 'Monteiro block' method. This method uses small square blocks on which the child counts to ten. When the child reaches the tenth block, it is no more a unit number and has to be made into a decimal point, so we write one again because the decimal unit becomes zero. No school ever teaches us why ten is written as one and zero, so this was really engaging for me as a parent since I had never thought of such things.

By 2010, the new school, called Rishi Gurukulam, was up and running at Katarkhadak. Operations commenced with just a 3000-square foot hall, with an attached kitchen and external toilet block. Learning, playing, eating and sleeping... everything happened in this one hall. Today, this hall is used for SSY advanced meditation workshops (AMC).

The first few days at Katarkhadak were so much fun. Guruji used to involve the children in every activity. If any child found the road mucky, he told them, "Don't complain, make the path yourself." All the youngsters, including Vedoci, had a blast laying bricks to make the road.

A lot of emphasis was on practical learning. Even a field trip to nearby caves would be followed by children enacting a play or making a presentation in the caves.

The lodging, boarding and tuition fees added up to a modest ₹ 10,000 a month per child, with no hidden costs. Today, five years later, this amount is ₹ 15,000, which makes it one of the most affordable residential schools in Maharashtra. Other residential schools charge no less than eight lakhs per annum.

In Rishi Gurukulam, kids are taught to work as a team. No element of competition via ranks is encouraged. Also, most processes are made fun. For example, until seventh standard, children are allowed to set their own examination papers, with teachers selecting one question from a bank of questions given by each student. This gets them involved and still leaves them with no option but to study the entire syllabus.

As soon as we shifted Vedoci there, I changed my mode of working.

I divided my week into two halves. I visited the Baggit head office Wednesday through Friday. Saturday mornings were allocated for retail store visits for customer interaction. This perfectly took care of the work front.

Saturday evening, I drove up to Katarkhadak and stayed there until early Wednesday morning.

I had my cake, and devoured and digested it too. I managed my business and got to spend time with Vedoci and Manjo, as well as pitch in with school activities. Being the foodie that I am, I volunteered to manage the school's kitchen. I also began arranging for factory visits for the kids.

> "It had already been quite a struggle for Nina to accept Manjo moving full time into spirituality, but when Manjo suggested that even Vedoci should go to the residential school in Katarkhadak, it was shocking for Nina. While she relented, it is not because Manjo dominated her. She has always been flexible because she is courageous."
>
> *— Rita Lekhi,*
> *Nina's childhood friend and sister-in-law*

The beauty of the Katarkhadak hills mesmerized me. Whenever I went there, I swam in the backwaters of the Mandi dam near the ashram.

The school and ashram have an unobstructed view of the hills with stunning waterfalls finding their way through the greenery. It worked like a balm for my tired eyes.

Manjo built tree houses all over the premises. I started using them to do my paperwork in and was stunned at how quickly I got through them when I was there. The best ideas came to me in the silence of these mountains amid the sweet chirping of birds and shimmering insects.

My evenings at Katarkhadak ended early with the school *arati* sung by a group of little girls, including Vedoci. I joined Guruji's adventurous activities with the kids. I trekked in the surrounding hills or played football on a rainy day. I even began jumping off the nearby bridge into the water. Adventure is so much like entrepreneurship! I found challenges like 'taking the plunge' as crucial to business as they were to keep my enthusiasm alive.

Guruji's creative ways to spend every evening, and infectious enthusiasm, made me drop all my inhibitions. I began looking forward to getting back every week.

I rekindled my childhood love for cycling, and experienced the relaxation that had eluded me all my life. I learned to take a moment and reclaim my days. Earlier, time had just flown past me.

Even today, when I am with Vedoci and Manjo, I put my phone on silent mode and check it only after long intervals. I know no other way of giving them quality time.

But time does fly. Vedoci is now in the tenth standard.

After only five academic years, Rishi Gurukulam has 100 students. A lot of parents also choose to live and teach at the school.

Nina working from her tree house at Katarkhadak

Cycling in the picturesque Katarkhadak.

Playing with the kids at school

Two children from our school earned a CGPA of 10/10 in March 2015 and were congratulated via email by the Human Resource Development (HRD) minister, Smriti Irani. A few of our secondary school students also participated in the National Finance Literacy Test 2015. They topped the Western Zone and were felicitated by the Deputy Governor of the RBI.

LEARNING:

Increase your range of happiness.

Manjo keeps asking all those who attend SSY workshops, "What is your range of happiness?" People are so scared to step out of familiar boundaries. They say things like, "We feel very cold when the temperature is below 22 degrees, and very hot when it's above 26." This means that they can be happy only within a range of 4 degrees.

Similarly, I had resisted change, thinking I could only be happy in the same house, same suburb, and same city.

Choosing not to send Vedoci to Katarkhadak would have resulted in her playing with a gadget in the evenings, rather than climbing a tree. Also, I would probably have cholesterol issues and be forced to attend endless meetings at the office; let alone cycle in the hills with Vedoci. Did I do well by changing my old habits, and increasing my range of happiness? I think I did!

8

Stitching the SSY Culture into Baggit

Siddha Samadhi Yoga, founded by our Guruji Shree Rishi Prabhakar, infused miracles into my personal life, and I felt its magic in my professional life as well.

Ever since I began SSY meditation, I have felt more calm, capable and decisive. Following SSY teachings consistently over the years has had an even deeper impact. I was able to get rid of certain harmful behavioural patterns. I think that I have become a better person.

My worst trait, my temper, finally came under my control. When we were dating, Manjo used to call me 'KiFi' (kiss and fire). He would say, "I just don't know how you can be so cute one minute, and blow your head off the next!"

This was true. I had suffered and caused suffering all my life, thanks to my temper.

In the year 2010, Manjo began conducting inner transformation workshops known as SCOPE. SCOPE stands for 'Silence, Clearing, Organising, Planning and Energising'. This is a practical workshop that focuses on techniques to get rid of behavioural habits. It is designed to fix big egos and make people realize that they are nobodies in this infinite universe.

I attended the workshop that focused on making and breaking habits. In the first hour, we learn to accept the fundamental truth of Vedantic philosophy: you are responsible for everything in your life. You can decide which habits you want to get rid of or create. Once you decide to get rid of a bad habit, there are repercussions to not keeping your promise. I promised that I would control my temper; but, like any old habit, it was not easy to break.

The consequence of losing my temper was that I would force myself to eat only raw food (really tough) for two days. Everyone in office was a witness to my pledge.

Three workshops later, however, I still could not rein in my temper; so, despite my Sindhi genes – which naturally gravitate towards fries – I ate raw food for two whole days. The next time I had the urge to yell, I stopped short. The person I was mad at started looking like a plate of raw food to me. The voice inside my head said, "Swallowing anger is way easier than swallowing salad."

This experience made me understand one thing about anger. We lose control because we feel there is nothing to lose when we do. But when there is an immediate and personal consequence, we don't make that mistake.

"Nina ma'am Superwoman hai. Kabhie break nahi leti. Maine dekha hai, jaldi gusse mein aa jaata hai madam, tabhi saamne wala thoda apne acche ke liye shaant ho jata hai... Phir jab bhi madam ka mood accha hogaya, to unko vaapas bulaake problem solve kar deta hai!"

(Nina ma'am is Superwoman and never takes a break! And I've seen that she gets angry easily. So for his or her own benefit, the other person becomes quiet. Once her mood improves, she calls them and solves the problem in no time.)

— Subbaiah Naidu,
Nina Lekhi's chauffeur for 15 years

After this, it has become much easier for me to handle people. I now think of myself as an MD who inspires rather than instructs.

In 2009, Manjo gently hinted that I should share Guruji's teachings with each of my employees. I readily agreed. We were lucky to be assisted by a very well-read, spiritual SSY *sevak*, Ghanshyam Dariyani. He helped us ingrain the SSY culture into Baggit. Mr. Dariyani even worked out a schedule to ensure every employee attended SSY programs.

However, nobody has ever been forced to attend these workshops. I personally explain to the staff that there is no ulterior motive in making them follow SSY. We only want prosperity and harmony for all our employees.

> "Nina herself is genuinely committed to SSY as she wants to see that all of her employees grow internally, as they grow professionally. She bears 100 percent expense for the same. It's a huge cost to give leave and pay for the program. Baggit also loses man-hours because Nina gives additional holidays to make up for the days spent in SSY workshops. She wants all employees to be happy individuals, not just stressed workers meeting targets."
>
> — *Ghanshyam Dariyani,*
> *Chief Spirituality Officer, Baggit*

My staff began going for 'silence workshops' for three days every two months.

These are days when they are told to avoid communication with the outside world. They experience firsthand how silence leads to heightened creativity and joy. The staff is also encouraged to attend other SSY programs, as per their needs. One such program is SSY Emotional Insights, which helps people understand their personalities and take charge of their emotions.

We soon began conducting SSY workshops in our factory premises when employees could not visit Katarkhadak.

Mr. Dariyani recently launched the Fun Club or *Satsangs* for one hour once a week. These are not religious exercises. They are just group activities and games to bring teams together and improve intra-team bonding.

We regularly take feedback from our staff. They have been very positive about these workshops. If an employee refuses to go for workshops, it is not held against him or her; but the fact is, most of them enjoy it. They also know that, apart from Baggit, huge companies like BilCare Ltd (a 4000-crore company), Mahesh Lunch Home, and even the Star Group, send their staff to Katarkhadak for these workshops.

I have also created fixed meditation slots at intervals throughout the day in office. Whether people meditate or not, the company provides the time for it. Additionally, twice a day, at company expense, healthy snacks such as nuts and salads are served to the entire staff.

As for me, I became more generous. I started sharing part of my profits with my employees in the form of

Nina and Manjo with Guruji

loyalty awards. I deposited a significant amount in the bank account of each of my employees to acknowledge their relationship with us. The amount was proportionate to the number of years they had worked with Baggit since its inception.

"I've been with Baggit since the time I finished college, but I had avoided the SSY culture for the longest time. By default, I was a tense person. Whenever there was a payment issue with the buyer, I used to call up Vicky and he was always relaxed. I just couldn't understand how anyone could be so relaxed 24/7. The difference was that Vicky had imbibed the SSY culture. He told Nina about my anxiety and she told me to go immediately for the silence workshop. Those three days in Katarkhadak, there was a halt in my life, like a person who has gone into coma. All activities stopped; I was with myself. I realized that nothing is more important than oneself. I now regard work as play. That's the difference in the culture of Baggit and other organizations."

— Vishal Ahuja,
Head of Operations, Baggit

I stopped thinking about competition, and it became effortless for me to regard even competitors as my friends.

Since 2009, I have seen my teams become more harmonious and confident.

"There is an enormous positive change in Nina. While she was always spontaneous and exuberant, there is a noticeable expansion in her being; a new consciousness she's radiating. Earlier, very naturally, she was not very open to discussing work, since both of us are in the same line. But today, she helps me in every possible way."

— Meera Mahadevia,
MD, Meera Mahadevia Luxury Handbags since 1985

About four years ago, my new HR head Sushma Sahai suggested that we offer full cover Mediclaim to all employees. I was easily convinced because this would be a great gift. Sushma said we could consider it for the next year, since Diwali was just three days away, but I moved heaven and earth to ensure it was implemented the same year.

A few months later, I heard my staff complaining about weight gain. They did not have time to go to a

The Baggit team during a silence camp in Katarkhadak

gym. That week, I got one of our existing *galas* converted into a gym and another one into a yoga room. Now, my HOD's think twice before conveying to me something that employees want. They know I will get it done right away and it could lead to lot of internal shuffling and shifting between *galas*.

For example, once Baggit's entire top management team went for a swim to Mandi Lake after completing a workshop at Katarkhadak. We happened to discuss work there. Suddenly, somebody commented that it is so relaxing to conduct meetings in a lake. I saw Vishal swim close to that person and say, "Be careful of what you say. If that reaches Nina's ears, another *gala* could be sacrificed to make a swimming pool." Then he looked at me and said, "Nina, it's just a joke – don't start building one!"

Thanks to my experience of living in Katarkhadak, I took the first step toward fulfilling my dream to create jobs for rural India in 2012. I created a rural manufacturing unit of 2000 square feet and hired workers from the Katarkhadak and Mann villages. All those who joined this unit had previously been going to cities, and living difficult lives, away from their families for regular income.

As an entrepreneur, I promised myself that I would, in my own small way, reduce India's dependence on China in terms of manufacturing and slowly move all manufacturing processes to nearby villages. It is my dream that for work, rural Indians should never be compelled to leave their fresh mountain air, water and space, for the wretched standard of living that metros offer them.

Astonishingly, just as Manjo predicted, this initiative led to the kind of prosperity I could never have imagined. Baggit had been growing every year since 1988, but in the next chapter, I talk about how my business has grown 14-fold in the last five years.

It will not be wrong to state that whatever I have done for my employees, for the SSY ashram, and to create rural employment, has come back to Baggit in the form of blessings. Society (in the form of customers) has returned my wealth multifold, through unshakable loyalty to my brand.

LEARNING:
Visualize and manifest your future every two hours.

These are the teachings of an American inspirational author called Esther Hicks.

Esther Hicks conceived a powerful concept called 'Segment Intending.' She explains that any individual can decide how their life is going to be, and plan it down to the next two hours. This is because each individual creates his/her world through the mind. By visualizing everything, what you are going to do, how much fun you will have, how you are going to handle tricky situations, you can shape your entire future. I have always done this even as a teenager without knowing what I was doing. And Baggit is witness that it really works!

I have visualized my brand growing in leaps and bounds and wished the same growth for my employees, vendors, partners, buyers and even customers.

9

Getting into the Big League

Phase 4 of Baggit: 2009- 2014

Our exclusive outlet at Atria not only got us noticed, but also made Baggit a name to reckon with. It gave us the Midas touch.

Prior to our Atria store, buyers were always negotiating on margins, asking for the world. But the phenomenal success of our first store ended the haggling overnight. Our next EBO (Exclusive Brand Outlet) was a franchisee store at Matunga. Even though a friend owned it, the transaction was totally professional.

Shortly after, we opened an exclusive store at Linking Road, Bandra, a place where all big brands aspire to be. This was another milestone for us.

In 2009, after 25 years of relentless hard work within

the borders of Mumbai, we opened our third EBO at Garuda Mall in Bangalore. Luckily for us, the franchisee owner, Sabrina, was a very ambitious woman. She wanted to do much more than one store. This store did well too, and we soon tied up with three different Lifestyle outlets in Bangalore on SOR (Sale or Return) basis.

> "When I invested, there were only seven stores. Nina personally set up these stores, as she had no VM (visual merchandising) team. But everything has changed over the last decade. From being people-dependent, Baggit has transformed into a thoroughly professional brand."
>
> *— Sheetal Manghnani,*
> *owner of Baggit Franchise outlets, Mumbai*

So, while the new EBOs at Matunga and Bangalore ran smoothly from day one, the flagship Atria store had a few hiccups, because it was in a spanking new mall. Unfortunately, Atria had no multiplex or anchor store (e.g. Cinemax or large-format stores which draw retail traffic even to the smaller stores). The walk-ins were limited. After a year, big brands enrolled too, which increased foot fall to our store tremendously.

As we were learning more about stores, I realized

retail was a completely different ball game. We had been manufacturers or business-to-business (B2B) traders until now. We were used to making goods, and it was not our headache to focus on sales and marketing once we had sold them to wholesale buyers.

Our buyers like Shopper's Stop and Lifestyle carefully analyzed which variants sold well, and gave bulk orders for the same. Now we, too, had to learn that art.

One concern I had was that if a particular style was selling well in Bombay and Bangalore, the purchasing department of the large-format store blindly bought the same style for their outlets in other cities as well; however, there are many differences in terms of bag requirements between different states. I realized that people in different cities, zones, and localities have different preferences.

For example, in college areas or IT hubs, we found differences in the types of bags that people demanded. Those residing in the central part of a city used different bags compared to those who lived in the suburbs of the same city.

Delhi requires a different handle size, because the shoulder size of North Indian women is taller than average. In the South, pastels don't sell as much. We have research and hard numbers to prove this.

I advised my teams to begin work on capturing these nuances.

I also hired Ashwini Gulanikar, for my organization to

learn more about the business of retail. Armed with new insights, we began advising our buyers. We also started making products along the same lines.

"Our retail consultant taught us this fantastic concept called 'Velocity'. This simply means 'Rate of Sale' of a product. It is calculated on the basis of how many pieces of a style are sold per day, per store, within a fixed period of time. At a glance, Velocity reports indicate whether a style is bread-butter (a core style) works for us or needs to be faded out. Earlier, we used to come up with an approximation. Now we know exactly how much sells, in which city, and even to which age group!"

— Vishal Ahuja,
Head of Operations, Baggit

The retail consultant, Ashwini, suggested a big change. Within her first week of joining, she told us that we were neglecting the huge potential of 'shop-in-shops'. We already had many counters in Pantaloons, Benzer, Amarsons, Shopper's and Lifestyle, but very few shop-in-shops.

Before Baggit attempted it, bags as a category were never sold on SOR (sale or return) mode. This model was available for branded apparels and footwear. But never bags. So, acting on the consultant's advice, we approached our oldest buyer: Shopper's Stop. We asked them if they were willing to convert the Baggit counters in all their stores into shop-in-shops. They were reluctant. They said it might not make a difference.

I cajoled Shopper's to give us only one location to pilot this. Since we had a great rapport with them, they agreed. They allowed us to conduct a month's trial in their Malad (Mumbai-North) store, which had the most foot fall. We spent on the signage and fixtures, and replicated the look of our exclusive stores. This was in the last month of the year 2009, and we made a whopping profit of eight lakh rupees in one month at this store!

Shopper's Stop was elated. Now they insisted we convert all our counters nationwide into shop-in-shops. At that time, they had approximately 25 branches. Our business actually grew three times just with Shopper's Stop!

Then we repeated this model with Lifestyle, Pantaloons, and Central.

The entire bag industry followed suit.

I remember that our retail consultant was pushier than I am (if that's possible!). She drilled into us the desire to add more EBOs and work on our brand presence, so I leapt into the world of business plans. Suddenly, phrases like 'projects teams' entered my vocabulary. We set a target number of store openings for the year, and it was a hell of a lot of work. We already had too much on our plate, so we initially tried to outsource the store furniture and fixture work, but it was too expensive. To allow us to do things ourselves, I created in-house projects teams.

For once after giving birth, I lost weight without going to the gym. I was running to and fro trying to augment production to meet the ever-increasing demand for our products – besides opening stores and managing them.

It was time for a retail team. Until now, the designers for each Baggit product were taking care of merchandising as well. Now, this was no longer possible because there were too many stores to manage. We needed systems in place.

Backend operations had become less people-dependent about eight years ago. We knew what an advantage it was to note what was sold and when to plan the next round of manufacturing.

Now, from approximating demand based on informal feedback, we had to organize formal weekly order reports. Almost overnight, Baggit recruited hundreds of front-end and back-end staff to man the new shop-in-shops all over India. The front-end staff needed more training. We needed to ensure that all salespeople embodied the Baggit brand personality: 'urban, helpful and fashionable.'

Salespeople can be a tricky bunch. Their jobs are one of the toughest and require a lot from them. Some take their roles lightly and need to be supervised closely. The evening shift staff cannot leave until the store closes its doors. They must appear well groomed and hygienic, wear branded uniforms and communicate effectively. And, most importantly, they must reflect a sincere intent to help every customer. Those who are genuine need to be motivated and rotated to avoid burnout.

Once we got the retail department in place, we started hiring Area Sales Managers. ASM's would ensure high-quality service in every city. We hired them first for South India since we had a greater presence there, and then for the North; but when the business grew even bigger, we hired regional managers to supervise the ASMs.

I had neither an MBA nor any mentors; I learned on the job. Except for listening to my father's narration of his nice and not-so-nice experiences as an entrepreneur, I had no training in running such a large business.

Today, I realize that the incidences I heard from dad are the very things taught 'theoretically' at B-schools, as case studies. I've hired kids with MBAs who are sometimes clueless about handling practical situations, whether with a client or a worker.

That is how a proprietary firm like Baggit rose to the next level. New systems and processes, all newly learned, made the whole transition happen seamlessly.

Getting Baggit to such heights was a dream I dreamed along the way. Each member of my team put in a lot of hard work to make sure that whatever we did, we did well.

In 2009, Shopper's Stop awarded us the Highest Selling Brand in the category. The very next year, we were recognized as the Best Retailer in the category by Inorbit Mall, Hyderabad. By the end of the same year, we had reached the magic figure of manufacturing – one-lakh bags per annum.

Challenges

Opening new exclusive stores has always been exciting, but was never easy. In 2008 and 2009, we decided to move North. The first store location we zeroed in on was in Delhi NCR (Gurgaon) in a mall. We signed a big store of 6000 square feet, which was very expensive to rent; however, this mall had Lifestyle as its anchor store, where we additionally had a tiny 125 square feet shop-in-shop counter. We were selling a good number there. So, in spite of the high rent, we thought that if we were performing so well at Lifestyle, we would sell at least two and a half times as much from our own exclusive store. It was a calculated risk.

As soon as we opened the Gurgaon store, after spending so much on the interiors, the market crashed. Recession had hit the country. This store was the most expensive store we had signed. Other brands started renegotiating the rentals and the store owners supported them to the extent possible.

We re-negotiated only in those stores where our sales had dropped drastically. Our Gurgaon EBO (exclusive brand outlet) was one of them. To say that we were bleeding financially is an understatement. The store owner reduced our lease amount for a few months by a very tiny figure. It didn't help us. After a few months, we requested him to renegotiate, as sales had still not picked up; but he didn't consider our request. That year, Baggit as a company made the least profit of any year yet, and we were aware that it was due to that Gurgaon store.

We were locked in for three years as per our agreement and had paid six months' lease amount as a refundable security deposit. Worse, our post-dated cheques for three years were lying with the owner. We met a few lawyers to see if there was any way to exit this situation legally. The exit clause in the deed said that if we vacated the property before time, then not only would we lose our handsome deposit amount, we would also have to pay the lease for the remaining lock-in period. All the lawyers advised us to get out of the property and then challenge the owner in court. They said that this would change the game because the owner would surely choose to avoid litigation.

We were in a dilemma. On the one hand, our entire company's profits were being eaten away by this one store. On the other was the commitment of signing a legal document. I felt that if I had signed an agreement willingly, then I should remain committed to it. That was my value system, and I was not going to let an external economic circumstance compromise it. I requested my top management team to look for new ways to reduce cost and improve profitability or sales. That year, my top management team refused to take any increments in salary.

Post the lock-in period, the owner agreed to reduce the rent by 50 percent. We ran the store for two more years and exited the mall, as it had lost its popularity. New malls opened up close by and we moved there.

LEARNINGS:

Always have an exit strategy before starting anything.

I learnt so much from the Gurgaon store experience. The new set of rules when it comes to leasing are clear in my head:

Never sign a lease agreement with a lengthy lock-in period, and don't issue long phase post-dated cheques towards rent. Before entering any discussion on renting or buying a property, a thorough cost analysis should be done. This means that I must know how much my rental budget can stretch. Heavy rentals can completely change the business scene if projections go wrong. I have also learned to always do a thorough assessment of the sales potential of the brand stores next to the property that I want to lease. This usually gives me great insight into what my sales projections should be. Finally, I always think of my exit strategy when I am planning my entry.

10

... Bigger, Biggest!

Meeting the demand of one lakh bags was impossible without automation.

We had already taken a baby-step towards automating manufacturing processes in 2007. To speed up the process of cutting, we had bought a few semi-automatic machines called clickers. These helped us reduce wastage and improved the look of our bags.

However, any manufacturing business is dependent on many factors. Sometimes, it feels like whack-a-mole. You have this big hammer, you feel you are in control, and you hammer with all your might – but you just can't guess where the mole is going to pop up next. One must be alert and keep a vigilant eye on the quality of inventory, the machinery and the worker. Most importantly, one should always plan ahead. Within two years of buying the clickers, we needed to produce even bigger quantities. I had to keep many things in mind before I invested in newer technologies.

> "There are several advantages associated with automation besides quick production. The main one is the reduction of wastages. This is not only environmentally friendly; it also reduces the cost of the final product."
>
> *—Vishal Ahuja,*
> *Head of Operations, Baggit*

Production is a cycle of five elements: quantity, quality, cost, time and new inventions. We needed to constantly ensure that these were in control. Earlier, Baggit only had teams looking after overall costs. Post 2009, when competition intensified, I created more layers to ensure that we remain efficient so that the cost of bags does not increase. I elevated Vishal to the head of production. Below him, I added team leaders for the entire production cycle.

For these people I set KRAs (Key Result Areas) because timelines, quality, quantity and cost are all interrelated. Every little bottleneck had to be captured and checked.

The fifth and the most important part of production is new inventions. To keep up with our global competitors, it is very important to keep our ears to the ground for new machinery and techniques.

By 2011, I felt that neither the numbers nor the designs I wanted could be created without spending on 'fully-automated' machines. I wanted a certain quality of bags, which was not possible with the infrastructure that we currently owned.

> "Earlier, the franchisee had a free hand to decide what to stock or not; but now, Baggit has strict policies and guidelines about merchandise. Also, earlier I could just call Vicky (from Sales) to send me more mobile pouches. But now there is a separate department for replenishments and for customer care, and I cannot call one for the other. This level of professionalism has only made it easier and made all of us richer."
>
> *— Sheetal Manghnani,*
> *owner of Baggit franchise outlets, Mumbai*

Vishal, then VP Operations, and Vijay, VP Production, combed machine fairs for the latest technologies. It was a huge expense to upgrade, but we could not afford to hesitate. We replaced eight clickers with big state-of-the-art cutting machine – so big that they consumed whole *galas* at Narayan Bhavan; however, no one from production wanted to dump the old clickers, so we kept two of them for nostalgia and backup. We think of them as important stepping-stones in our growth story.

While all this was going on, we kept pushing for new EBOs. 2011 saw the opening of our tenth EBO. We were meeting our annual target of stores with all the 360-degree detailing required. We now focused on hiring international experts to imbibe the best global practices in manufacturing and retail.

Through this journey of expansion, I have had many moments of doubt and fear, but every time I feel myself getting disheartened, something good always comes my way.

In 2007, Baggit won the Peta Proggy Award for endorsing 'Fashion without Cruelty.' This award meant so much to me, because it validated my commitment to never use leather for our bags in spite of what the competition was offering.

In 2012, another huge honour was bestowed on me – the Karmayogini Award by Maharashtra Economic Development Council. This was in recognition of the exceptional work done by women. I was felicitated by Chief Minister Prithviraj Chavan for being an active champion on the social, economic and governance fronts. This was in recognition of our welfare initiatives, especially the work we do with our employees in our spiritual workshops. The award also recognized Baggit's contribution to creating rural employment.

At the same time, Baggit India became a private limited company and from being proprietor I became an employee on a salary. The designation I chose for myself was 'Creative Head.'

In terms of market value, we became a 50-crore brand. By December of the same year, we had opened our 30th exclusive brand outlet and started selling in Kenya.

In 2013, a long-cherished dream came true. We started selling in the U.K. I was very sure that my relentless envisioning of having a Baggit store in the UK had materialized.

We started retailing through our own E-Commerce portal (baggit.com), as well as through online stores such as Flipkart, Myntra and Amazon. The markets we reached by selling online were way beyond anything I could have imagined.

In July 2015, I was sitting in my office when a stray thought entered my mind. It had been a long time since Baggit had won an award. Magically, just minutes later, I got a call telling me that Baggit had won an award from the Ministry of Micro, Small and Medium Enterprises.

I took my entire family with me, including Manjo and

my in-laws, to Ahmedabad to receive the award. I knew that without their support, I wouldn't have been able to achieve so much. I can recreate the moment every time I close my eyes, of myself standing on the stage, in a blue *saree* with Manjo in a red *kurta* by my side, receiving the award from SME Minister Kalraj Mishra. It was surreal.

The next time I felt this way was when Vedoci and Manjo accompanied me as I received the Outlook Business 'Women of Worth' Award in October 2015. What a moment this was! Outlook is a magazine that features people I have always been in awe of. Even in my wildest imagination, I would never have thought of sharing space with them. I requested Manjo to join me on stage as I had to speak about the one person who inspired me to achieve so much. Vedoci was over the moon that I won the award along with her favourite actor Deepika Padukone.

Our Facebook fan base grew to over five lakh people by the end of 2015. It felt as if even in the online world the skies had opened up for Baggit.

Challenges

As any organization grows, many (unwanted) systems are required to maintain the same energy levels, which had required no effort when it was tiny. Two years ago,

Nina at the MSME award function

my HR head and I faced opposition towards the KRAs that I set for all teams. I understood that it was difficult to migrate to the concept of KRAs, because Baggit was not such a formal organisation earlier.

I addressed my entire company at once. I explained that the *raison d'etre* for KRAs was that if Baggit's vision was to be achieved, it needed to be broken down into goals and small steps that could be measured as KRAs. And if KRAs were worked on responsibly, then nobody would need to sit on anyone's head or push them. If each individual started achieving his KRA, then Baggit as a brand, and employees as individuals, would win together.

To the collective pain of all my staff, Sushma, our Head of HR also implemented a new Balance Score Card (BSC) method of appraisals. My teams informed me that 30 percent of their time was being used up creating those quarterly reports, so I asked my team to make the reports departmental, instead of individual.

I also told the departments that if they wanted to scale up, like the international brands we collectively swoon over, they would have to work with the same precision that their parent organizations do. I think that certainly struck a chord.

Finally, nothing works like discipline. All Baggit employees have witnessed, first hand, how following processes in all departments has led to the growth of the organization, resulting in super plump pay packages.

Now everybody loves KRAs and reveres them as another form of Goddess Lakshmi.

LEARNING:
We're all connected.

I follow Joe Dispenza, a well-known author and lecturer who has explained, in simple steps, how everyone can access a healthy and fulfilling life. Dispenza uses the principles of Quantum Physics that have proved that everything in this world (including humans, animals or even the desk in your office) is a vibrating form of energy. Of this energy only 0.000001 percent is matter. On breaking down every human cell into atoms, and further into protons, neutrons and electrons, it was found that they were made up of constantly-spinning vortices of energy. Each energy field radiated its own signature, which could be good or bad energy. Even with energy, like attracts like; and good energy attracts good energy.

I applied this thought to my stakeholders. If all of us are intrinsically the same vibrating matter, then I should focus on being a good person with a positive vibe. Being honest, genuine and friendly in my dealings has always attracted genuine staff, buyers, and vendors. What Joe said proved true, and actually worked for me.

11

Marketing, Movies and Masala

As Baggit stores opened all over the nation, and the brand grew in stature, we had to invest in making noise to get noticed. It was time to invest heavily in marketing.

With every new store opening, the company spent a lot towards advertising and customer interaction. In 2008, we conducted a huge marketing campaign with international star Freida Pinto. We also created our corporate website, including our entire product catalogue, and built an in-house social media team that would focus on developing our digital presence.

In 2012, during a holiday abroad, Vedoci, just in her teens, mentioned to me how she loved the Victoria's Secret store. I was stunned because my daughter, who obviously didn't understand retail the way I did, was indirectly commenting on the ambience of a store. She had even noticed the fragrance inside! This was the impetus for me to redesign Baggit stores.

This, however, was not an overnight decision. Foreign brands such as Zara and Mango had entered India, and their store formats were interesting and different. I had also been traveling frequently to the East at the time, and was keenly studying the ambience and décor of the stores there. I realized our product was far above the current ambience of our stores, designed many years ago.

I had been on the lookout for professional agencies that could help us change our retail identity. In spite of identifying a foreign retail design firm, I had been a bit hesitant. Not only because of the sizeable amount I would need to pay for their advice, but also because of the concerns we had: Would a foreign agency understand our market? What sensibility would they bring? What if we don't like their suggestions?

When Ken Nisch, chairman of JGA Inc. called us into his office in Detroit, all my doubts finally withered away.

I had taken my entire design team along so we could all learn together. Ken was surprised to see eight of us arriving at his office. Our visit was fruitful and rather educational. He took us around New York City and Detroit over two days and explained design elements of a variety of stores. He showed us how brands such as Abercrombie were offering two completely different retail experiences in two different cities. In addition, he made us sensitive to the attention needed on window displays. Not too many Indian brands (and definitely not a single Indian bag brand) regarded windows as integral to the retail experience. Abroad, however, the creative drama on store windows was breath-taking. I was ready to embrace the big changes he suggested for Baggit.

> "What is unique about Nina is this combination of energy and innate intelligence. Having worked with her, I learned that, without having a formal education in IT or an MBA, she is able to grasp the essence of what management issues in large organizations are. She may not necessarily have the answers, but at least she will ask the right questions. She is always open to learning new things and to hiring experts. That, and the unique combination of how she endears herself to people, is just amazing."
>
> *— Sanjiv Shah,*
> *SSY teacher, close friend and now technology consultant, Baggit*

Ken overhauled our store design and retail identity, and made us redo every little detail. He suggested that our salesmen wear black blazers and the saleswomen, halter jackets. For packaging, he asked us to use the colours light aqua blue and chrome orange.

In terms of the layout, he advised us to go for a library fitment format, i.e., library-style shelving as we needed to display many more products or SKUs (purchasable items with an alphanumeric numbering) as compared to international brands. It was what the Indian consumers wanted and Ken's suggestions were outstanding! These metallic shelves were ingenious because the customer could view one item and all of its variations in a single glance.

"Nina has worked hard to build the Baggit brand. She has worked with the best photographers and models right from the initial Baggit advertising campaigns. She dedicates a lot of her time to brainstorming new ideas for advertising and Brand Vision. She is a dear friend and we've had many discussions about Baggit's marketing. I have always respected Nina for encouraging free-wheeling and democratic discussions across teams when it comes to marketing. Normally, this sort of thing doesn't happen in large organisations."

— Deepali Naair,
Close friend and marketing advisor to Nina

Baggit revamped: The store design that Ken Nisch conceptualized.

He also told us to paint our front wall a bright orange to attract customers walking outside, and that this wall to go all the way to back of the store. There was a glow light on the floor of every shelf to accentuate the bags on the lower level.

Our predominant brand colour changed from browns and whites to a lively orange! Overnight we had an international look, which was well received by our customers and got us many more walk-ins.

In 2012, with the energy that trying something new gives one, I also dared to attempt something we had never done before – to tie up with the biggest made-in-India marketing tool: Bollywood.

Not one to settle for the small fry, I agreed to tie up with one of Bollywood's biggest films, *Bang Bang*! The movie was touted to be an official remake of Hollywood's *Knight and Day*. The lead roles featured Bollywood superstar Hrithik Roshan and Katrina Kaif, and the deal was brought to Baggit by Sapna Ahuja (who was our head of marketing then).

We were all pepped up when we signed the agreement with Fox Star Studios, but the movie release was delayed by a whole year, from 2013 to 2014. We had known theoretically that a delay could happen, and it was mentioned in our agreement, but somehow we had not anticipated it.

We had produced the new styles to be used during filmmaking, and we put these products in stores at the time the film was originally expected to release, in 2013, as we couldn't hold on to ready stock. The bags sold well, but we lost the advantage of being able to launch a new collection along with the movie.

The second disappointment was that the placement of the bag in the movie was on a 'best-effort' basis. We were all very excited because, during discussions, it had been agreed that our logo would be shown clearly; however, we felt it was a blink-and-miss appearance at the end of the film.

This deal taught us that, despite contracts and agreements, if the movie director felt that any scene does not suit the film, he could alter or remove it. It was nobody's fault. Finally, when the movie actually released in 2014, we re-launched some of the bags from the collection in stores. But the movie did not turn out to be as big of a success as we had hoped, so it didn't help sell many bags then either.

When working with Bollywood, the ultimate success of an unreleased movie is a bet that you are making, and sometimes you lose that bet. But, like I said, the 'Bang Bang' experience made us much smarter. It was a tough lesson to learn that when tying up with external organizations to launch a collection, a lot of things remain beyond our control and all eventualities must be planned for. We are much more careful when entering into any association now.

Our production and publicity teams have also started thinking long term. For instance, our marketing team plans strategies, campaigns and photo shoots for two seasons at the same time. Our production team plans for collections 18 months in advance! It is all about playing the life game.

The year 2014 ended as beautifully as it started: we opened our 40th exclusive brand outlet with a bang (bang)!

> "Nina has this amazing ability to let go of an experience very easily, in the sense that she's willing to not hang on to things. She can take things in her stride; when something exciting happens, she will celebrate it. And then she's not stuck on that. She's able to move on to the next. Her excitement is unfettered by what others think. That's why she is able to do things which are different."
>
> *— Devaang Shah,*
> *Financial advisor & Nina's cycling buddy*

The *Bang Bang!* experience gave my marketing team more confidence. We used all these lessons as we began planning our association with India's premier fashion event: the Lakmé Fashion Week (LFW). We were the official Bag Partner for LFW 2014, and it was really big for us. The partnership materialized thanks to Nucleus, our PR agency. To see Baggit branding all over Fashion Week made my heart swell with pride. The immeasurable impact of such a glamorous event was exhilarating.

After winning hearts at Lakmé Fashion Week in 2014, I decided to make a splash at the LFW in 2015. I hired dancer-actor Lauren Gottlieb to debut at the LFW as showstopper for Baggit. The whole show was beautifully stylized by accessory designer Little Shilpa.

I also took up the challenge of losing weight before the fashion show. For a month, I worked out twice a day and went on a strict diet, as I visualized myself matching steps with Lauren on the ramp. Not to mention the endless behind-the-scenes work of launching our next season's products. I was elated with the gains of the rigorous pain that I put myself through.

Lauren's talented catwalk spiked with her famous dance moves lived up to all our expectation, as she launched Baggit's new Autumn-Winter collection. I held my own in a little blue dress, another of my long-cherished dreams, as I walked the ramp with her.

But what made me happiest was the media coverage

Nina walks the ramp with Lauren Gottlieb at LFW 2015

Lauren Gottlieb with the core Baggit team at LFW 2015

and applause that our new collection, titled 'The Rusted Revolution,' received.

I had personally designed this new collection. My nervous steps on the ramp took me back to the year 1984 where the 17-year-old me craved appreciation for my new set of bags. I was over the moon as I soaked in the applause received by Baggit. I guess some things never change.

LEARNING:

'Whatever you focus your attention on, grows.'

It feels clichéd to say that every failure is a stepping-stone to success, so I will just stick to my favourite affirmation coined by well-known spiritual author Louise Hay: 'Whatever we focus our attention on, grows.' The Bollywood deal was very expensive. It was a first-time experience for us, and we were nervous as well as excited. We didn't know the right questions and we were afraid to ask. As eager by-standers struggling to break into the glamour industry, yes, we got a raw deal.

But why should I focus on that? I will focus my attention on what we gained rather than what we lost. We learned how to work with Bollywood. That is a big deal, and there will be so many new opportunities, so many magical associations to look forward to. In the future, if we pay money, we know how to get the bang for every buck!

12

Family in Business and How We Made It Work

Anyone who has visited the head office at Baggit asks me the same question:

How come there are three family members in my top management team? And how do I make this work?

Hiring family members in my organization was neither consciously planned nor avoided. Decades ago, when I asked my brother Mukesh and first cousins Vishal and Vicky to work with Baggit, I had absolutely no idea that we would grow so big.

All of us were young and inexperienced then, and we took every day as it came.

Like anybody else, I worked best with people I trusted. I never thought about the long term, except to pay salaries responsibly every month.

It has been wonderful to build a brand from scratch

Nina and her cousin Vicky, hard at work.

with my family. We have also had our own share of challenges, which would have occurred whether or not we were related. I'd like to summarize it this way: Baggit grew with Mukesh, Vishal and Vicky, as much as they did with Baggit.

> "Nina used to pay me about ₹2500 per month in the late 90s, and this was great money for an 18-year-old. After a year, she didn't give me any increment because she felt I was doing time-pass. She was right. Once I became serious about work, I had great growth. Throughout my 18 years with Baggit, Nina has treated me as a cousin only at family functions."
>
> — *Vicky Ahuja,*
> *Head of Marketing & Sales, Baggit*

Since childhood, I have been close to my brother and cousins. I thought of them first when I needed help. They were also eager to help out during the initial Baggit sales. I sincerely paid them the best stipend I could afford. Our transactions were always professional.

The culture among Sindhis is such that business is considered way more glamorous than jobs. Mukesh was really good at academics. After graduating as a Science major, he pursued a diploma in Marketing from NMIMS (Narsee Monjee Institute of Management Studies) in the late 80s; but he was not keen to join our father's manufacturing unit in Mazgaon.

This is because dad's life was truly tough. His daily routine involved visiting factories, taking orders and getting them done via workers. In spite of all that hard work, dad struggled with credit transactions all his life.

My maternal uncles were into retail and that looked like much more fun. Mukesh loved visiting their air-conditioned offices at Lamington Road, where they sold imported tape-recorders and VCRs.

He felt that that was the good life: *A/c dukaan hona chahiye, jahaan* (there should be an air-conditioned shop, where) one can just sit and earn hard cash.

This prompted him to start INXS – his retail store at Kemps Corner. Since he chose to retail bags and accessories, only girls visited the store. If there really was a heaven, Mukesh had found it in his shop.

We had a deal that I would give him a better margin on the bags I made. He reciprocated by coming to my factory to give us design input once a month. By and by, he began helping with merchandising and production planning, i.e., how many bags of a certain design should be made in which material.

These early days of Baggit are etched clearly in my

memory. I will never forget that Mukesh was Baggit's first hard-core supporter. And his INXS was Baggit's first exclusive retailer.

For 15 years, until 2003, it worked like this. By 2007, he started coming to the office once a week. As the organization grew, the hierarchy fell into place. I made sure that Mukesh spearheaded the design team because he was born design-savvy. After a couple of years, Mukesh became the head of design and merchandising and joined Baggit full-time.

"It is not true that being in a family business makes people irresponsible. Whether in Baggit or my own business, I have found family more responsible, as they value everything as their own. Nina commands loyalty because of her warmth and love for people. Also, nobody has ever thought, 'Hey she is a lady boss.' The entire staff unanimously regards Nina as *'sab ka baap'* (everyone's pop!)."

— Medu (Mahendra Karkera)
Nina's close friend and proprietor of
Mahesh Lunch Home

Vishal, who was 18-years-old at the time of joining

Baggit, assisted Mukesh in managing INXS for half of the day. He worked with Mukesh for five years, until he graduated in commerce and got married.

I remember calling him on the second night after his wedding (thankfully, I left him alone on the first night) and asked him, "Now what? You must take more responsibility." I told him to join the Baggit factory full time and look after wallets. Vicky and Vishal initially worked on anything I requested them to. Slowly, they gravitated to lead the functions they were best at.

Vicky, too, was barely 17 when he joined Baggit. He was great with people from all walks of life. When a retailer arrived, he would attend to him. When a worker came, he commissioned work to him. He also managed petty cash by collating bills from everyone.

I never told him to run after retailers, saying, "*Yaar, itna manufacture kiya hai, do ya chaar piece aur le lo*" (We have manufactured so much, please take two or four more pieces).

I never wanted Baggit to be about the short-term. We always gave good advice to those who bought from us. I remember initially telling everyone who worked with me that if a certain design is not selling we must be honest about it.

Vicky used to tell buyers, "Sir, *yeh* design slow *hai*. If you still like it, take one piece… try if it sells. Only then take large quantities."

Thus, he cemented a beautiful rapport with buyers. In no time, they began trusting him implicitly. Soon they began telling him, "*Yaar* Vicky, just choose and send." These relationships became our biggest assets.

At the same time, I'd noticed that Vishal, who was Mukesh's protégé, had a thorough understanding of systems and processes. He had done a splendid job with wallets. We used to manufacture only 250 wallets per month when Vishal had joined in the late nineties, and he brought that figure to a whopping 35,000 in just a few years. He was young blood, proving to be a worthy successor to Mukesh. I soon realized that Vishal was a people's person too and could convince anyone to accept his point of view.

As Baggit was growing rapidly, we soon needed an Operations Head. I felt Vishal was my best bet to manage this responsibility in the future. About two years ago, I told Vishal to head Baggit Operations, with immediate effect. He moved seamlessly into the new role.

Recently, I have had disagreements in office with someone very close to my heart – Mukesh, my darling brother. The issue was minor, but became larger than life because of the quick growth that we have been experiencing. As head of design and merchandise, for him, work suddenly changed from small to extra-large in size.

Over the last decade, merchandising as a whole has undergone a metamorphosis and turned into a very complex science. In fact, the whole retail industry has evolved so much that we collectively drop our jaws every few weeks.

For example, we recently launched a haversack purse. We needed to stock enough sizes and colours in all stores. Trend analysis also suggested that we needed more options, such as drawstrings instead of zips, in some models. We also needed to offer colours that are in trend. For instance, metallic colours were big in autumn and winter 2015. All our large-format stores and exclusive stores needed to be sent the correct numbers in the right mix. And everyone knows that it is not possible to track 300 stores accurately without automating our systems. To make all of this happen, every season is planned 18 months in advance. That is the level of effort required to hook and retain today's discerning customer.

Mukesh found it overwhelming to plan in advance. I felt upset with this because if Baggit slipped anywhere, someone from the competition would happily meet the customers' needs.

Mukesh has always been the smarter sibling between us and is good with analytics; but he needed to become more detail oriented, and I kept pushing him to do so. So, last year, I suggested that Vishal temporarily help him out.

"I started my career with Mukesh and he was my first boss. I know his strengths and weaknesses. And he knows mine. We have reached these heights because of his team and him, and I know that even in the future we will work together beautifully."

— *Vishal Ahuja,*
Head of Operations, Baggit

Once again, Guruji's teachings showed me the way out of this conflict. I simply had to see the godliness or the potential in the other person rather than focus on what I was not getting. Guruji always said that it is the entrepreneur's job to stop the buck from being passed around. In Baggit or in any other company, appointing a new person looks very easy, but it is not. Before breaking something, I felt why not repair it?

I realized I was pushing Mukesh towards merchandizing, whereas his strength lay in designing. It was my KRA (as MD) to recognize his strengths and give him an assignment where he could use them. He is now in charge of designing and executing the new 'Nina Lekhi Premium Range.' He is the most experienced person in Baggit's design team and he loves the new role. A problem that could have become a full-fledged family row was thankfully resolved with a change in my mindset.

> "Baggit has grown in leaps and bounds in the last few years and the new processes take time to get used to. Nina and I have come out unscathed through bigger trials, and are going to resolve any issue in the future too. SSY has taught me that I attract any positive or negative experience with my own thoughts. The circumstances around me are created by my inner world, so I had to change myself first. Also, our goals are bigger than both of us. The goal is 'Baggit.' Nina found a solution, and I am keen to live up to her expectations."
>
> ***— Mukesh Punjabi,***
> ***Nina's brother, Head of Design & Merchandise, Baggit***

I'm also delighted by this turn of events because Mukesh is my brother second and my work soulmate first. Baggit would not be where it is without him. He has always been by my side and has handled all of his responsibilities beautifully since the inception of Baggit. And so it will always be.

I'm always open to discussing and listening to any differences of opinion in Baggit. I want every member

> "Everyone asks me this silly question, about how Mukesh, being the elder brother, feels about reporting to his younger sister. But I always tell them that between Akbar and Birbal, it was obvious that Birbal was the cleverer one. So then how come he never became the emperor? In other words, ***'sab ke naseeb mein sab nahin hai!'*** (Everything is not included in everyone's destiny). It is also your past karmas. Also, being the Managing Director of a company does not necessarily make you the happiest person.
>
> As Nina's mother, I can also see the heavy burden she carries on her shoulders. In spite of being the MD, she remains the same person she was as a child – super honest and super giving. She keeps nothing for herself. Look at the simple house she lives in, or the unpretentious car she drives and you will understand."
>
> ***— Gita Punjabi,***
> ***Nina's mother***

of my staff to be comfortable expressing how they feel while working with me – and my relatives should share this comfort. It makes us more vibrant and effective as an organization. If everyone becomes a yes-man, our competitors will have the heartiest laugh. And no true-blue Shikarpuri Sindhi in my family is going to let that happen. There is nothing that a lovely lunch of Sindhi Curry and fried *aloo* (potato) cannot resolve between all our relatives. Oil-is-well! ☺

LEARNING:

We are all part of a larger family.

Guruji has instilled so many values in me, one of which is to always regard myself as a parent – not just towards my biological child, but the entire world, starting with those working in my organization. This means that whenever they make a mistake, or don't live up to my expectations, I must treat them not as my employees, but as my children. So just the way I accept a mistake made by my child, I should accept others as they are. It creates mutual love and acceptance, and sets both sides free. And suddenly achieving the work objective becomes easier than ever.

13

Business with Love

For a business that has grown from scratch over 25 years, a lot of our suppliers and vendors have become close friends. A lot of people issues, which we hadn't anticipated, keep surfacing. We try to take everything in our stride. This usually happens because Baggit is growing by leaps and bounds, and the way we worked earlier doesn't work for us anymore. For example, we used to work with a single vendor. Today, at the scale we have achieved, it is impossible to rely on a single vendor for anything.

Rajesh Mehta or 'Raju,' my raw material supplier from day one of Baggit, is a family friend and also a gem of a person. He works only from his heart. Earlier, it used to make sense for me to work like this. He was my only vendor in the initial years. Even in the late 80s, when we were doing about 30 lakh of sales annually, an unanticipated delay by Raju would cause chaos.

"Nina is always in this position, where, most people who work with her are extremely close to her. Not just family or friends, even total strangers who join Baggit and attend SSY spiritual programs become attached to her. This is because she cajoles them to grow spiritually. However, Nina doesn't let this comfort allow anyone to take her for granted at work."

– Manoj Lekhi,
Nina's husband

With experience, I decided as a policy decision a few years ago to keep two vendors for all purchases. As the Managing Director of the company, it was my job to manage and minimize risks. My policy is to give Raju a larger share but not all of it. I decided on a share of 70 percent for Raju and 30 percent for the others. He believes I give him lesser than what I claim, and I cannot do anything about his belief. The 30 percent is just to give us a buffer and avoid panic. If I don't maintain this, I will not be able to face the 800 full-time employees who work with me. If they are answerable to me, I am also answerable to them for their job security and career.

Today, Baggit's operations have become so big that I cannot meet everyone in person for every decision. A lot of things are happening on email and text, and, understandably old friends and partners like Raju resent this.

> "I worked with Nina for 20 years because when I worked with her, I never felt that I was doing business. I always thought with my heart. When Baggit had just been launched, I willingly lost money for 10 years. Today, I feel betrayed because Nina's Baggit is now so big and she charges me a penalty of ₹2 lakh a day if I deliver late. I also find it difficult to access her now."
>
> *— Raju Mehta,*
> *family friend and vendor of*
> *raw materials for Baggit*

At our current size, I do not permit any internal person or department to unilaterally change a plan without discussion, no matter how brilliant their idea is. All departments are interlinked and a small change gets everyone entangled in the mess.

Baggit has always vouched for every fitting, material and adhesive used. We have recalled a product if something has gone wrong. Caring for the environment and our customers is very high on our list of priorities. We have almost zero percent wastage because we use leftover material to make bags at the villages in Katarkhadak. Baggit has always committed to ensure in-house repairs for its own bags (which very few brands do) and we also recycle our used bags.

Hence, I have requested all my vendors (including Raju) to conform to international quality norms, as this is what our customers expect. I simply cannot compromise on the quality of bags. As a brand, I can't tell my customer, "Oops! The material came from China, so not my fault!"

I am sure Raju feels betrayed that I do not give him 100 percent of my business like I used to, but I have no choice. I can only hope to be understood – I cannot change a business decision that is necessary to ensure Baggit's survival and success.

Challenges

Any organization will have a few bad seeds. Long ago, I set a rare example by asking some people to leave. One was the head of my accounts department. For eight years, he misappropriated funds via checks claiming business purposes. We found out through bank reconciliation statements. He confessed in confidence to my CA. I waited for him to confess to me, but he didn't. Once his corruption was proved, I had no choice but to let him go.

Another employee, who currently works in the purchase department, has been rumored to have accepted kickbacks for years. I still trust him because I have no proof, and I choose to think positive.

In the case of poor performance, I always encourage the employee to go for training. Sometimes there is no chemistry between two people in the same department, which causes friction. At Baggit, the SSY workshops help immensely in bridging these gaps.

My rate of firing employees is legendary because it's even lower than Baggit's attrition rate. The few times that I have sacked someone, it has never worked for me.

In my experience, when you fire a person, you will also lose a person you want.

Once, when I removed somebody who was cheating me at Baggit, I soon also lost two lovely people who were great team players. I was visibly upset and Guruji told me that this happened because of karma. He explained to me that there is no next life – you settle all your accounts here only.

That does not, however, mean that I suffer negative people. Those whose actions have consequences on innocent people are gently asked to instantly reform or leave. When it comes to minor disputes, I follow another solution given by Guruji, which I have shared with you.

LEARNING:

Practice the Ho'oponopono – A timeless Hawaiian healing technique for healing and forgiveness.

In business, as in life, it is possible that people make a wrong decision due to lack of information. I am very sensitive to this. If I sack someone due to a mistake in judgment, I will never forgive myself.

How I behave with say, Vicky, I must behave with Vijay from production, or anyone else. Otherwise, all my spiritual work is just pretense.

I aspire to give Baggit employees the feeling of togetherness that exists in a large family. Where mistakes are forgiven and forgotten, and any member of my staff feels safe to recount their weaknesses to me – like a child would to a family member.

I also follow the 'Ho'oponopono' which can be simplified as the four mantras of 'Sorry, thank you, please forgive me, and I love you.' I learned this in an SSY Scope workshop.

Just by uttering these four *mantras* in any situation, you cause people who don't match up to your vibration or energy to either transform or drop out of your life on their own. It also gives one the power to simultaneously transform oneself for the better.

You have to believe it to experience it.

14

What's Next?

Since 2012, I have gotten my second line of management ready. All my Heads of Department have complete autonomy to make decisions.

Vicky is looking after sales and marketing; Vishal beautifully orchestrates operations, and Mukesh gives his innovative spin to Baggit designs every season. Our CFO, Anand Navalkar, ensures improved profitability by making sure each of us is aware of our financial ratios.

Today, 33 years after my neighbors yelled at me because of my *ghar-ka-factory*, I operate from 45 *galas* in the heart of Mumbai. Baggit is present in 61 cities, owns 40 exclusive brand outlets, and is available in 300 multi-brand retail stores.

We now hire 800 full-time employees and 850 contract workers, who work together to launch six new collections every year.

I wish that everyone who works with us aspires to achieve great things for Baggit. Personally, I want to work harder to actualize new EBOs (Exclusive Baggit Outlets), which I have visualized in every country of the world.

We are soon integrating all our systems into the new ERP (Enterprise Resource Planning) software. I have engaged experts in most areas to assist my top management team in making the transition to bigger numbers. We have Sanjiv Shah for technology, Pradeep Java, our new CIO (Chief Information Officer) who is helping us collate Business Intelligence and getting our CRM (Customer Relationship Management) software in place.

Because Baggit was incorporated on November 2, 1989, this year we are also celebrating the 27th year of 'Brand Baggit'.

I have decided to focus solely on creativity and inspiring my team, as I step back from operations. I am eager to chalk out the future growth of my brand, by leveraging our experiences and the things we have learned into bigger numbers and wider geographies.

Maybe, I'm finally ready to say the words... Baggit is no longer my little baby.

It is now a responsible, well-earning, adult organization with a vibrant future. It has just earned permanent membership into the 100-crore club.

And there is so much more to pull out of the bag...

Baggit Fundas

Change is the only constant: At Baggit, we believe in this age old maxim because that is the way life is. We apply this concept to people-management, our stores, and our products. We keep changing the job profiles of our team members to keep them challenged and interested. I dislike doing one thing for too long. I believe the best way to motivate executives is to rotate them and allow them to understand how different departments work. Similarly, I also think customers need change, which motivates us to constantly ideate and produce new bag designs all through the year to exceed their expectations.

Eat the frog: I believe that every workday can be broken down into smaller steps. To give an example, the day can be broken into 10 important tasks to be achieved. Out of those 10 things, I push myself to complete the worst one first. Author Brian Tracy says that, "If the first thing you do when you wake up in the morning is eat a live frog, then nothing worse can happen for the rest of the day!" Thus, we enhance our energy and momentum for the rest of the day. Failing to do so makes us focus on other unimportant duties, which drains energy. Eating the frog results not only in effective time management, but also makes every day productive and goal oriented.

Growth and inclusion go hand-in-hand: I am focused on the wellbeing of not only our management executives but also our labour force; they are the strength behind our growth. Whenever I make a business decision, I keep the end result in mind and plan backwards to implement each step in detail. Nothing is ad-hoc and out of the system and no team is taken by surprise. For example, whenever I have a new idea to augment operations, I explain to the operations team the 'why & how' of making it happen. Once they feel included and understand what is expected, as well as how to do it, quantity of output is never an issue. I leave it to them, and the feeling of inclusion works for all of us.

Well-planned, organic growth: Today when we open newspapers, we hear about big brands suddenly opening 500 stores overnight. While I do have huge plans for Baggit, I have chosen not to hurry, and focus more on detailing and customer satisfaction, as that is what has brought us so far. Baggit's growth is therefore organic and will never be an overnight decision to reach certain numbers. Once I have made a decision to do something, I look at all the things required to implement it and then estimate a timeline. The decision could be opening a store or phasing out a *gala*; for example, we shut a *gala* in Hinjewadi (Pune), which wasn't working for us. I am balanced about both ends of the spectrum.

15

Me at a Glance

Short-term Goals

Professional: Generating employment in rural areas. I call it short-term because I have set a short time frame for myself to implement this. I have already started, with my first rural unit at Katarkhadak in 2012.

Personal: To lose another 10 kilos of weight and experience every adventure in sports. To be calm and loving towards all. To see godliness in every living being.

Long-term Goals

Professional: I want Baggit to contribute its bit to improving the currency imbalance between India and the developed countries.

Personal: I want SSY's Rishi Gurukulam at Katarkhadak to inculcate the culture of silence in the children who study there and this can be done via workshops. I don't want anybody to suffer like I did – to have to work so hard to rid my mind of its baggage in order to be at peace.

My Favourite Brand: It was, is and always will be Topshop from London. My friends often tease me if I am ever lost in a city abroad, I can easily be found at the Topshop store closest to my hotel. It has been my dream to have my store in Oxford Street and earn back all the money I have spent in pounds during my trips. I'm sure I'm getting there soon.

Most Inspiring Book: *Jonathan Livingston Seagull* by Richard Bach. It's a book about a seagull that never stops learning. This book's wisdom connects with what Manjo teaches at the SSY SCOPE workshops.

Most Inspiring Movie: *3 Idiots* for its message: do what you love and love what you do. It shows us how enjoyably enlightening education can be. Kids do not thrive by cramming theory, even though they get high scores. Life is about being able to adapt to situations and still get stuff done.

How I Unwind: Cycling, swimming, meditation and adventure sports. I love cycling outside the city to new destinations. Any outdoor activity with children is very energizing for me.

My Success Funda: Anybody who has done real business knows that great relationships with the people you work, passion for what you do, generosity and detachment towards money, comprise the tested formula for success.

Dress Code: Comfortable tee and torn jeans. I still shock my head of HR.

Relationship Mantra: Being honest, loving without hesitation, and clearing any grievances by communicating openly. I learned this early on from my friend Mana (actor Suniel Shetty's wife) who taught me this in college. I was upset with her during our screen-printing class, and gave her the cold shoulder. She was not sure what had gone wrong, but she still approached me and sorted it out immediately. I have followed her mantra all my life.

Biggest Thrill: Seeing yet another woman carrying a Baggit bag. Feels the same as a teacher giving me marks in school. *Goosebumps*

Biggest Strength: My ordinariness. I do not claim to be a genius and I'm very comfortable in my skin.

I think I am street-smart, humble and therefore open to learning from anyone who is willing to teach.

Biggest Weakness: Spilling the beans for a good laugh. When Sapna joined Baggit 14 years ago, I forgot to pay her a salary for four months! When I realized, I immediately told her I'll give you ₹5000 per month. Five minutes later, my general manager Sudhirbhai told me, "*Usko kya zaroorat hai pagaar ki; woh toh Mahesh Lunch Home se hai*" (Sapna's father owns the popular restaurant Mahesh Lunch Home)! I couldn't stop myself from sharing this with Sapna, even though it was in front of Baggit's well-wisher, Sudhirbhai. Thanks to this, nobody tells me anything they don't want others to hear.

Peculiarity: Extremely extreme. If I work I can do it for 40 hours at a stretch. If I dance, I can dance till I fall. They say the pendulum has to go both sides. For me, the pendulum goes to one side and stays stuck there.

Advice to All: If you have a passion, pursue it. It will be tough. There will be days when you have lots of money and days when you have nothing in the bank. But you will be happy and sleep well. Work will be like play. And you will never ever need to drag yourself out of bed.

Acknowledgements

Nina Lekhi

I take this opportunity to thank those who helped in writing this book, by giving their accurate perspectives of my life and Baggit's history.

My adorable mother Gita Punjabi, who taught me to just give and give wholeheartedly.

My loving in-laws, Ved (Mom) and Jivan Lekhi (Daddy), who have treated me like a beloved daughter.

My husband Manjo, the most adorable and balanced man in the world.

Darling Vedoci, my little girl, who makes me look at life afresh!

My dearest brother Mukesh Punjabi, who helped me from day one, at Baggit.

My best friend cum sister-in-law Rita Lekhi from whom I have learnt so much.

Cutest Yo! bro-in-law, Dev Lekhi.

Brilliant Monica Lekhi (sister-in-law), for knowing and encouraging me all these years.

My dearest cousin Vicky Ahuja, who knows what I am thinking, without me having to say it.

My darling Sapna Ahuja, whose alignment with me is precise.

My dearest cousin Vishal Ahuja, who is a big family man and knows how to take everyone along...

Dearest Anita my cousin and also my efficient Executive Assistant, for mothering me.

Dearest Raju Mehta my family friend and material vendor for Baggit since many, many years.

My best friend Mahesh (Medu) Karkera, with whom I see the comical side of all situations and people.

My elegant designer friend Meera Mahadevia.

Sanjiv Shah, long time SSY friend, now my stronghold on IT in Baggit.

My dear friend Devaang Shah, who always gives me financial insights at a macro level, whilst cycling with me.

Ex-designer at Baggit, Sheetal Manghnani and who is now a Baggit Franchisee.

Close friend, Narendra Rane, who is a part of our team that runs the Katharkadak school and village projects.

My buddy Devangi (Tiny) Parikh for those wholesome and funsome (college) days.

Anand Navalkar (CFO, Baggit), whose team and his love for numbers fascinates me.

Sushma Sahai (Head of HR, Baggit), whose systematic approach to setting policies and systems has taught me a lot.

Vijay Mudaliyar (Head of Production, Baggit) for showing unstinting loyalty towards the brand and India these last 25 years.

Sudhir Mistry, for being our Rock of of Gibraltar.

Dear Deepali Naair, my friend, for helping me make the initial roadmap for Baggit's marketing department.

Ghanshyam Dariyani, our Chief Spirituality Officer.

A big thank you to Suman Chhabria Addepalli for the bond created between us, while writing the book.

And last but definitely not the least, my indispensable man-Friday, (Sarthi) Subbaiah.

A heartfelt thank you to all of you and many others who have been part of this long and beautiful journey. This book would not have been possible without you, and I absolutely love each and every one of you!

Suman Chhabria Addepalli

One can never really fit all the details of a person's life into 100 odd pages.

Especially that of someone who founded a business as a teenager and inspired all the men in her family to be part of it.

I had the time of my life connecting with Nina. At first, her phone was either busy or unavailable. But I quickly built a rapport with her six assistants, through whom I could reach her. I soon realized that Nina's demanding schedule didn't offer a moment of respite.

Even so, I followed her through high and low-pressured days, to find her ever lively and positive.

Cheers to the God of Coincidences as not only is Nina a Shikarpuri Sindhi like me, but also an alumna of the school I attended. Every interview with her, was punctuated with school banter, laughter and delicious Sindhi food.

All my love to Nina, for embracing me as the co-author for her book.

Gratitude to Manjo, for rightly convincing me to attend many SSY workshops to really understand the philosophies Nina has incorporated into Baggit.

I feel blessed to have acquired an assignment which handed me all of Guruji Shree Rishi Prabhakar's philosophies and books on a platter.

I also want to thank Nina's family, friends and colleagues for generously sharing their vibrant perspectives.

Gratitude towards Rashmi Bansal, my friend and founder of Bushfire Publishers LLP, for believing in me and giving me the opportunity to write this book. My special thanks to the co-founder of Bushfire Publishers, Niyati Patel, for her discerning feedback on every chapter.

Special thanks to the publishing team at Jaico.

I would also like to thank my parents and siblings for their constant encouragement. Your love kindled my desire to express.

I wish to dedicate this book to the love of my life and my closest friend Srinivasa Addepalli. Without getting mushy, I can safely say that this book would not have been possible without your unconditional love and generous soul. And to our beautiful daughters: brilliant Leela (my most lovable, loyal, encouraging fan), and adorably elegant little Koel (who loves me the way one should be loved: for just being me).

This book was conceptualised and written under the supervision of Rashmi Bansal and Niyati Patel of Bushfire Publishers. Our mission is to co-create compelling start-up stories and business biographies for CEOs.

Glossary

Thelas: Bags
Satsangs: Prayer meetings
Gasar-gundi: A style of bowling used in gully Cricket.
Vela: Free or unoccupied (slang)
Chamchi: Teacher's pet (slang)
Behenji: Plain Jane (colloquialism)
High funda: Difficult (colloquialism)
Darzi: Tailor
Tagda: Hefty
Galas: Factory unit
Lambi Race ka ghoda: in it for the long run
Siddha: One who is spiritually accomplished
Pheras: The 7 'rounds' that a married couple must walk around a sacred fire during a Hindu wedding ceremony
Mahurat: Auspicious time
Daadhi: Beard
Lungi: Sarong
Chidia ghar: Zoo
Chaddar-ka-jhula: A swing made from a bedsheet
Bada: Big

Chhota: Small
Istriwala: The neighbourhood launderer
Pukka: A proper tar road
Ghar-ka-factory: Garage startup
Ghar waapsi: Homecoming

JAICO PUBLISHING HOUSE

Elevate Your Life. Transform Your World.

ESTABLISHED IN 1946, Jaico Publishing House is home to world-transforming authors such as Sri Sri Paramahansa Yogananda, Osho, The Dalai Lama, Sri Sri Ravi Shankar, Sadhguru, Robin Sharma, Deepak Chopra, Jack Canfield, Eknath Easwaran, Devdutt Pattanaik, Khushwant Singh, John Maxwell, Brian Tracy and Stephen Hawking.

Our late founder Mr. Jaman Shah first established Jaico as a book distribution company. Sensing that independence was around the corner, he aptly named his company Jaico ('Jai' means victory in Hindi). In order to service the significant demand for affordable books in a developing nation, Mr. Shah initiated Jaico's own publications. Jaico was India's first publisher of paperback books in the English language.

While self-help, religion and philosophy, mind/body/spirit, and business titles form the cornerstone of our non-fiction list, we publish an exciting range of travel, current affairs, biography, and popular science books as well. Our renewed focus on popular fiction is evident in our new titles by a host of fresh young talent from India and abroad. Jaico's recently established Translations Division translates selected English content into nine regional languages.

Jaico's Higher Education Division (HED) is recognized for its student-friendly textbooks in Business Management and Engineering which are in use countrywide.

In addition to being a publisher and distributor of its own titles, Jaico is a major national distributor of books of leading international and Indian publishers. With its headquarters in Mumbai, Jaico has branches and sales offices in Ahmedabad, Bangalore, Bhopal, Bhubaneswar, Chennai, Delhi, Hyderabad, Kolkata and Lucknow.

SINCE 1946